energy revolution

climate change and our post-carbon future

By young people of the world

A project of Peace Child International

PEACE
CHILD
INTERNATIONAL

Evans

acknowledgements

LEAD AUTHOR AND EDITOR: Joseph Lacey

GRAPHIC DESIGNER: Lewis Goodwin

GRAPHIC ILLUSTRATOR: Richard Lewis

PUBLICATION MANAGERS: Eugenia Capalbo, Joseph Lacey, Tanya Mowbray

RESEARCH TEAM: James Backham, Lotte Barron, James Freeman, Jasmin Geddes-Rainbow, Aoife O'Grady, Roisin O'Grady, Jack Owens, Charlie Parker, Alice Precious

PROJECT COORDINATORS: David R. Woollcombe and Rosey Simonds

EDITORS FOR EVANS BROTHERS LIMITED: Su Swallow, Sonya Newland

PROJECT CONSULTANT: Bart Ullstein

EDUCATIONAL ADVISORS: Roz Wilson, Jonathan Hart

WITH THANKS TO THE FOLLOWING EXPERTS WHO GENEROUSLY AGREED TO BE INTERVIEWED:

Fillippo Bernardi (Eco-securities), Sian Foster (Virgin Atlantic), Eric Hall (United Nations Framework Convention on Climate Change), Peter Lacy (Accenture), Mark Lynas (Author/Journalist), Per Meilstrup (Copenhagen Climate Council), Fred Pearce (New Scientist), Sue Riddlestone (Bioregional), Anthony Roberts (British Plastics Fed), Prof. Ralph Simms & Miika Tommila (International Energy Agency), Michael Stewart (World Skycat), Eliot Whitington (Christian Aid), Dr Gerry Wolff (Desertec).

PICTURE ACKNOWLEDGEMENTS:

UNEP 14, 17, 20, 25, 81, 82, 82, 85 (TUNZA)

Greenpeace: 30 (Markel Redondo), 32 (Greenpeace-Davison), 75 (Konrad Konstantynowicz), Istockphoto.com 19, 35, 53, 74, 81 Youth Artwork:Tewanat Saypan Taiwan 7, Charlie Sullivan UK 16, Luna Xinyuan Li USA 28, Amy Yun Zhang USA 39, Perettipon Yingthawon Thailand 48, Gloria Ip Tung China 56, Yeu Ching Nam China 62, Sien Diem Sione Malaysia 77. mnn.com 22, Solar Cookers International 33, flickr/madsprahm 34, flickr/tmaideramd 36, Pelamis Wave Project 37, Marine Current Turbines Limited 37, Corbis/ Kim Kyung-Hoon 47, The Volkswagon Group 49, Riversimple 49, City of Münster Press Office 50, HySolutions 51, Solazyme 52, Valcent Products 52, Eurostar 54, Peace Child International 59, Bioregional 61, EFDA-JET 66, flickr/ jujaz 76, flickr/Vevo Tubin 81, WWF 82, 350.org 83, Max Robson 84, plant-for-the-planet 84, carrotmob.org 84, Ryan Voarden 85, Energy Action Coalition 86, Robert van Waarden 86, Mike Rusell 87, Lewis Goodwin/Peace Child International 87.

Published by Evans Brothers Limited
2a Portman Mansions, Chiltern Street, London W1U 6NR, UK
www.evansbooks.co.uk

British Library Cataloguing in Publication Data
Energy revolution. : climate change and our post-carbon future
1. Global warming--Juvenile literature. 2. Global
warming--Prevention--Juvenile literature. 3. Sustainable
development--Juvenile. 4. Power resources--
Juvenile literature.
I. Peace Child International.
363.7'3874-dc22
ISBN-13: 9780237539627

Peace Child International gratefully acknowledges the support of the European Commission, DG Education and Culture in the preparation of this book.

Education and Culture

Youth

energy revolution

climate change and our post-carbon future

A project of Peace Child International

With contributions from young people of the world:

Susie Bowden, Julia Toro, Sarah Lacey, Felix Finkbeiner, Daniel New, Santiago Thibaud, Luke Cox, Bremley W. B. Lyngdoh, Esther Agbarakwe, Katla Björg Kristjánsdóttir, Hamza Khaleel, Richard Lewis, Isaac Musyoka, Tanya Mowbray, Eugenia Capalbo, Candia Crosfield, Joao Scarpelini, Robert van Waarden, Cast of Kids on Strike – Rocheser USA.

With special thanks to the participants of the European Youth Congress:

Rok Strohsack, Vivienne Wong, Timo Uustal, Rita Macskási, Jolanta Stoniewska, Zarina Niyazova, Hannah West, Dorottya Arvai, Ioan Cosma, Andrea Carafa, Nassim Djaba, Blaz Gasparini, Veerle Vrindts

contents

foreword

Congratulations to the young people of Peace Child International for creating this book – and thank you for reading it.

On the issue of climate change more than any other, it is young people who will see the effects of action we take now.

Children and young people know that it is not inevitable that we produce heat-trapping gases: we can have cleaner energy, easier public transport, and homes and businesses that don't waste so much power. By working together, we can avoid the dangerous effects of climate change and prevent the globe warming by more than two degrees. We can create a better quality of life and better communities.

Britain is committed to doing its bit. We have a sector-by-sector transition plan to create a low-carbon country – already, for example, we produce more offshore wind power than any other nation in the world.

We are arguing as well for a global deal that is ambitious enough to keep climate change below two degrees, and is fair between nations.

The energy and the optimism of children and young people are needed to make that transition happen. They are powerful advocates for change, and they can help turn their homes or schools into beacons of the new ways of living.

By learning about climate change, persuading others, and making change in our own lives, each of us can make a difference – and this book shows why that challenge is the most important that any of us face.

Ed Miliband

Rt Hon. Ed Miliband MP,
UK Secretary of State for Energy and Climate Change

introduction

'Now is the time to confront this challenge once and for all. Delay is no longer an option, denial is no longer an acceptable response. The stakes are too high, the consequences too serious.'

President Barack Obama

Stable weather patterns, reliable water sources, healthy rainforests and seas, and a diversity of plants and animals have allowed our species to flourish over the last several thousand years. Now, all this is threatened as our greenhouse-gas emissions warm the planet at a far faster rate than ever before, promising to drastically change the climate and endanger the very survival of our species.

And the good news? We can save ourselves. This book is not about how we could deal with the worst consequences of climate change through adaptation measures, like flood barriers and drought-resistant crops. Our purpose is to discuss how we can mitigate, or limit, the effects of climate change by tackling the deepest root of the problem: our greenhouse-gas emissions from burning the fossil fuels on which we have come to rely – coal, oil and natural gas.

This means building our post-carbon future – the world we could be living in by 2050, if the world unites to embark on the global energy revolution that will end our dependency on fossil fuels and change forever the way we relate to the planet and each other. And there's more good news – the ball is already rolling as governments, businesses, communities and individuals are taking great strides towards making the post-carbon future a reality.

This book is written at the early stages of the energy revolution and is intended to inform young people about what's being done, and what they can do, to accelerate the move to a post-carbon future. As with all revolutions, the pace of change is extraordinary. Some of the facts and issues have shifted alarmingly in the six months we have been working on this book. What hasn't changed are the three themes dealt with in the three sections of the book: 1) the problem: global warming; 2) the solution: a post-carbon future; and 3) how we can make this solution a reality.

What the post-carbon future will look like is not set in stone. Our generation will play a big role in making it happen over the next 40 years. We have been given the unique opportunity to lead a historic energy revolution and save the planet from catastrophic climate change. To advance that crucial goal, all of us at Peace Child International hope this book proves helpful.

Joseph Lacey
Lead Author and Editor

visions of a post-carbon future

In our lifetimes, everything we know will change because our civilisation is built on carbon fuels – oil, coal and gas – which are a finite resource. They will run out. And, if we burn them to the last drop, we will cause catastrophic climate change. To prevent this, our generation must build a post-carbon future independent of carbon fuels. It will cost us about US$45 trillion – about 1 per cent of our lifetime's global turnover. We believe we must do it, not because we have to, but mostly because a post-carbon world will be a great, clean, happy place to live!

In a post-carbon future, there would be electric cars around me, no smoke bursting out of exhaust pipes filling my lungs with disgusting gases. Bikes would swarm the roads, the landscape and forests would be pristine and filled with wildlife. I'd like to live there 'cos I'd feel safe there. I would know there will be a world to live for and that we could all plan our future without having to worry about dangerous weather conditions.

Luke Cox

UK

For me, a post-carbon future would be a time when no more oil is drilled, no more coal is mined and no more gas is piped in our planet. It would mean a time when all remaining fossil fuels are only burned with 100 per cent carbon capture and storage technologies. In a post-carbon future I see a world where apart from energy, no fertilisers, no plastics, no drugs, no foodstuffs – nothing will be manufactured from fossil fuels. As President Obama promised, 'I will create five million new jobs in the new green economy!'. Other politicians and leaders from around the world will follow his leadership, and within five decades they will create 500 million green jobs generating a global turnover of US$50 trillion.

Bremley W. B. Lyngdoh

India

to the future

A post-carbon future means finding new means of transport, learning to ignore advertising and buying less. This would lead to less stress, more contact with people and nature, less loneliness. Also more freedom to develop ideas, give the arts more value, go back to what really matters. If we get there – if we defeat global warming – it would mean that human beings have acted together as one family as never before in history. That's a future I want to live in. One where we see beyond differences and are at peace with nature and ourselves.

Eugenia Capalbo
Argentina

Africa's post-carbon future will be different because infra-structure costs are prohibitive and incentives to go green are nonexistent. Also, Africa has so many other challenges which, climate-wise, are mere preludes to the looming threats of tomorrow. The only way out is for Africa to elect transformational leaders who will put in place a green energy programme. But then where will they come from? Perhaps the young people, who constitute the majority of Africa's population. They are, already, an important force and partner in the field of global interdepend-ence. It follows, therefore, that youths are social actors who are capable of carrying out projects and programmes in the field of sustainable development. These young people will eventually be the leaders in the effort to create the post-carbon future in Africa.

Esther Agbarakwe
Nigeria

section 1

problem: global warming

what's going wrong?

*We're used to hearing about global warming and climate change, but what exactly do they mean? Our research team spoke to Fred Pearce, environmental consultant for the international science magazine **New Scientist**, to help get the facts straight.*

What is global warming? Can we be sure that it's happening?

Global warming means that, on average, temperatures at the Earth's surface (on land and at sea) are increasing. Recorded average temperatures show that the planet is now around 0.76°C warmer than it was at the beginning of the twentieth century. And we can see its effects with extraordinary events, like the melting of the Arctic, taking place right in front of us.

1979

2007

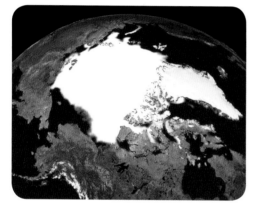
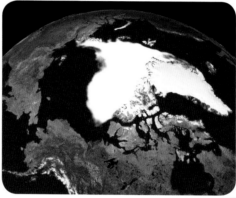

⬆ Temperature rise in the last 30 years has been enough to reduce the Arctic ice sheet by around 40 per cent, during its summer melt.

How does global warming relate to climate change?

The planet's temperature has a major effect on how the climate works, so a warmer globe means a changing climate (a long-term shift in weather patterns). Some examples of recent events indicating a change in climate are the New Orleans hurricane (Katrina), extreme flooding in Mumbai, prolonged drought in Australia, severe heat waves across Europe, and so on.

Has global warming really caused all of these extreme weather events?

Any weather event has a whole series of causes, so we can't really attribute particular ones directly to global warming. All we can say is that the recent period of global warming makes weather events like those I mentioned more likely to occur.

So what is causing the Earth to warm up?

That's the key question – it's mostly our fault. The greenhouse effect keeps the planet warm enough for us to live in (see below). By activities like burning supplies of coal, oil and gas, and cutting down forests, we send huge amounts of greenhouse gases into the atmosphere. In this way, we are thickening the blanket of greenhouse gases that surrounds the Earth, intensifying the greenhouse effect and warming the planet. Carbon dioxide is the main gas behind dangerous global warming, with methane a distant second.

The greenhouse effect

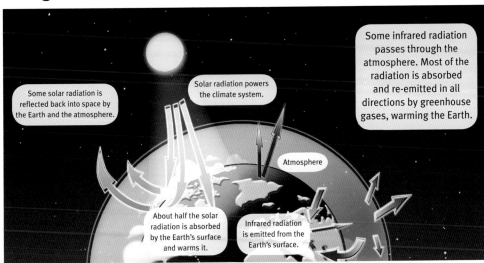

Some solar radiation is reflected back into space by the Earth and the atmosphere.

Solar radiation powers the climate system.

Some infrared radiation passes through the atmosphere. Most of the radiation is absorbed and re-emitted in all directions by greenhouse gases, warming the Earth.

Atmosphere

About half the solar radiation is absorbed by the Earth's surface and warms it.

Infrared radiation is emitted from the Earth's surface.

Could global warming not have some other cause than our greenhouse-gas emissions?

Aside from a stronger greenhouse effect, certain volcanic events and an increase in the sun's solar activity are just two other possible causes of global warming. But only our greenhouse-gas emissions explain the current period of global warming. It's very unlikely that these gases are *not* causing global warming and it would be very bizarre if they were *not* the result of human activities such as burning coal and oil.

Why do we hear doubts about global warming issues?

The probability that human activities have caused most of twentieth-century global warming is thought to be 90 per cent, so there is room for some doubt. Global-warming theory draws on lots of data from different areas of science, and many debates take place around it. Whatever scientists disagree about, the consensus is that today's global warming is happening, it's man-made and it's dangerous.

What do you think about global warming sceptics?

Honest scepticism is always healthy. It opens up dialogue and helps prevent people, especially scientists, from being over-confident and uncritical about how they understand the world. It's crucial, however, that we don't fail to take climate change seriously just because of some scepticism. The risks are too great.

the warming world

The heat is on! We're causing the globe to warm at an alarming rate by burning coal, oil and gas, and cutting down our forests as if there were no tomorrow. It's dangerous! Global warming of more than 2°C could put all our tomorrows on the line.

⬆ Every minute, an area of rainforest the size of 37 football pitches is destroyed.

Greenhouse gases

Carbon dioxide (CO_2 for short) is one of a cocktail of greenhouse gases – methane, nitrous oxide and others – which scientists measure under one heading of 'carbon equivalent'. In this book, we call it carbon because carbon dioxide is the main one. It comes from two main sources: burning fossil fuels (coal, oil and natural gas) and deforestation.

Fossil fuels

Fossil fuels come from the remains of animals and plants that existed well before the dinosaurs. Using oil to run our cars, gas to heat our homes, and coal for our electricity supply, we are burning up these one-time gifts from nature at a rapid rate. As fossil fuels burn, the carbon that they have stored for millions of years is released and combines with oxygen to produce CO_2.

Deforestation

Forests are one of Earth's crucial 'carbon sinks': trees 'eat' CO_2, store the carbon and release the oxygen. Destroying them has a double effect. When burned or left to rot, the carbon they were storing is released as CO_2. With fewer trees to absorb CO_2, more remains in the atmosphere.

Forests may be cleared for a number of reasons: so the timber can be used for fuel, paper and wood products, or to make way for roads, houses and farmland. As far as today's markets are concerned, forests are worth much more dead than alive.

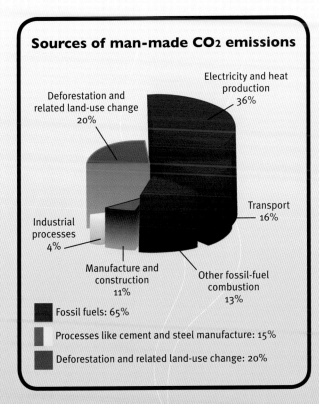

Sources of man-made CO2 emissions

Electricity and heat production
36%

Deforestation and related land-use change
20%

Transport
16%

Industrial processes
4%

Manufacture and construction
11%

Other fossil-fuel combustion
13%

Fossil fuels: 65%

Processes like cement and steel manufacture: 15%

Deforestation and related land-use change: 20%

Ragamuffin nature, tink again

All de people man dem, tink again
Before burning down de forest, tink again
Before to cut de trees man, tink again

Tink all da people or some o dem
Once de forest will go
de desert will come again
As de increase in de CO2 will make de
world hotter so making life some shorter

Man me say tink again, tink about de
desert de oxygen and de flower
all de people me say loudly, tink again

Amish K. Shah, Tanzania

Parts per million

One way scientists keep track of global warming is by measuring how many parts of CO2 there are in the atmosphere. For thousands of years, the concentration of CO2 in the atmosphere was at a comfortable 280 parts per million (ppm). Since industrialisation in the mid-eighteenth century, that figure has increased by more than one-third to around 390 ppm. That's bigger than any increase in CO2 over the last 650,000 years. Since the 1970s, we have been emitting CO2 at a ferocious rate, leading to a rise in average global temperatures of more than 0.6°C.

Two degrees

Average global temperatures do not respond to CO2 emissions for decades. Even if CO2 emissions were drastically reduced today, Earth would still be committed to about another 0.5°C of warming. Many scientists believe that going beyond a 2°C rise in global temperatures could have terrible and irreversible impacts on the Earth. To have a good chance of avoiding 2°C of global warming, estimates say that we must limit concentrations of CO2 in the atmosphere to 450 ppm. At the rate we are now burning up fossil fuels and wiping out our forests, we could overshoot this target in a matter of decades.

Questions and activities

1. Where does the electricity that your home and school consumes come from? Find out.

2. In 'Ragamuffin nature, tink again', what are the poet's biggest concerns for the planet?

3. Draw a picture to explain parts per million – the specks of carbon in the air.

Degrees of warming

Increasingly severe climate catastrophes could be the defining feature of our lifetimes. This is the least we can expect from global warming if we keep up with our greenhouse-gas emissions. Earth will survive, but will we?

Warming this century

Soon, we will reach 1°C of global warming. 1°C or even 2°C of warming may not seem like much. But if we consider that during the deepest freeze of the last ice age, average global temperatures were just 6°C cooler than today, temperature variations of a single degree begin to look a whole lot more significant. Climate-change expert Mark Lynas told our research team: 'At the rate we're emitting greenhouse gases, global warming of up to 6°C is possible by the end of this century, and we could be hitting 3°C of warming by 2050.' Six degrees, he says, is 'the difference between a habitable and an uninhabitable planet Earth.'

A hotter planet

Lynas became especially passionate about the issue of global warming at the turn of the century, after experiencing its effects for himself. 'When I went back to Peru where I grew up,' he says, 'the glacier I knew as a child had disappeared – completely melted.' This experience motivated him to write a series of books on the impacts and consequences of climate change, based on the latest climate science. In *Six Degrees: Our Future on a Hotter Planet*, he explains what each degree of warming, up to 6°C, is likely to have in store if we fail to adequately address the problem of global warming. Here's how he summarised things for us.

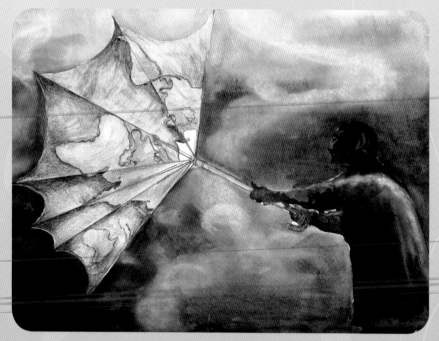

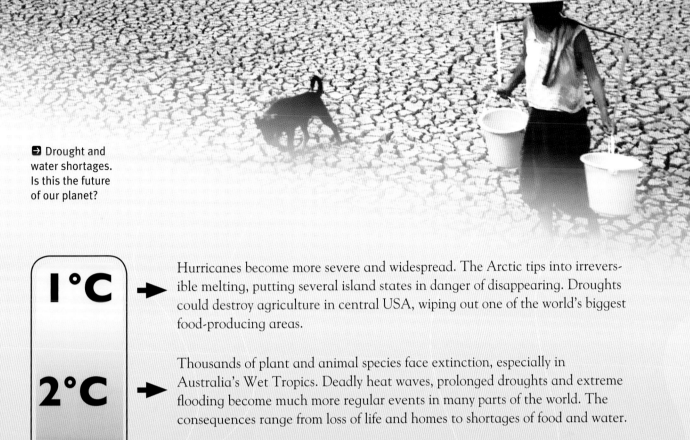

➡ Drought and water shortages. Is this the future of our planet?

1°C ➡ Hurricanes become more severe and widespread. The Arctic tips into irreversible melting, putting several island states in danger of disappearing. Droughts could destroy agriculture in central USA, wiping out one of the world's biggest food-producing areas.

2°C ➡ Thousands of plant and animal species face extinction, especially in Australia's Wet Tropics. Deadly heat waves, prolonged droughts and extreme flooding become much more regular events in many parts of the world. The consequences range from loss of life and homes to shortages of food and water.

3°C ➡ Drought and searing temperatures devastate the Amazon region. Declines in agricultural production pose serious problems with food supplies. Asia's major rivers lose much of their flow, resulting in water shortages. Up to half of today's plant and animal species become extinct.

4°C ➡ The Arctic has vanished; Greenland and Antarctica's ice rapidly melts. Sea levels rise by about a metre every 20 years, devastating coastlines. Worldwide starvation becomes a threat as droughts wipe out agriculture, especially in Central America, Africa, the Mediterranean, Southeast Asia and Australia.

5°C ➡ The world becomes unrecognisable from the way we know it today. Large areas of coastline are flooded; the rainforests are gone; major rivers have dried up; deserts are rapidly expanding even in Europe; the human population has greatly diminished; climate migrants walk the Earth looking for habitable lands.

6°C ➡ Scorching heat waves, stupendous hurricanes and fantastic floods are regular events in most parts of the world. Much of the Earth is unfit for human survival and every day becomes a struggle for those who remain.

Runaway global warming

Our CO₂ emissions are not the only thing that could warm the planet to 6°C. As we emit more CO₂, temperatures continue to rise and we get what scientists call 'positive feedback'. When this occurs, the rate of global warming rapidly speeds up.

Arctic melting

We have seen that warmer temperatures are melting the Arctic, but why is it melting so rapidly? Once some Arctic ice melts, it can leave large areas of ocean uncovered. Instead of the white ice reflecting away most of the sun's rays, the newly exposed area of dark ocean absorbs most of the incoming solar radiation. As the ocean warms, it contributes to further melting, leaving a greater area of sun-absorbing ocean exposed, which melts more ice, and so on. This is an example of 'positive feedback', a vicious circle that some experts believe could be unstoppable – causing the Arctic to be ice free in the summer months from as early as 2020. And without the Arctic acting as a giant solar mirror, the Earth will absorb more heat, pushing global temperatures higher.

> ### Did you know?
>
> In 2005 alone, the Arctic lost an area of ice the size of Texas or Afghanistan.

Death of the Amazon

The Amazon Rainforest runs through eight South American countries, serving as a habitat for an extraordinary range of animal and plant species while directly supporting the livelihoods and daily needs of millions of people. The great fear is that beyond 2°C of global warming, the Amazon will start to die as droughts and heat waves strike South America more frequently.

The gradual death of the Amazon Rainforest would deprive us of a highly important ecosystem and the service it provides as a carbon sink in absorbing massive quantities of CO₂. While collapsing, its 100 billion tonnes of stored carbon would be released into the atmosphere as CO₂, locking us into further global warming.

Ocean acidification

Around half of all our CO₂ emissions to date have been kept out of the atmosphere by a crucial carbon sink – the ocean. One important way it does this is through tiny plants called phytoplankton. Like trees, they absorb CO₂ to

⬆ Will the Arctic survive a 2°C rise in temperature?

grow, bringing the carbon they store with them to the bottom of the ocean when they die.

Absorbing such a massive amount of our CO_2 emissions has made the ocean more acidic – a change phytoplankton are finding increasingly difficult to survive. Fewer phytoplankton means that the ocean will not absorb as much CO_2, leaving more to be dumped into the atmosphere and driving up average global temperatures.

Carbon soils

The Earth's soils contain about 1,600 billion tonnes of carbon – more than double the amount now in the atmosphere – in the form of slowly rotting vegetation. Going beyond 2°C of global warming could affect soils in such a way that they begin to release this carbon more rapidly, causing a major acceleration in global warming. And the warmer it gets, the more rapidly the carbon will be released.

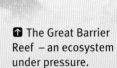
⬆ The Great Barrier Reef – an ecosystem under pressure.

This positive feedback could increase average global temperatures by several degrees, in which case the permafrost – permanently frozen ground – in Arctic regions like Siberia, Canada and Alaska would begin to melt. Around 500 billion tonnes of carbon are stored in permafrost soils – carbon that would seep into the atmosphere as the soils thawed, pushing global temperatures up by 6°C.

Meet Daniel

Located along 2,300 kilometres of Australia's east coast, the Great Barrier Reef is the most amazing coral reef in the world. As an Australian, it would be upsetting to see the reef become a victim of global warming. With warmer oceans and acidity levels rising, all it could take is a few more years of carbon pollution to wipe out this ecosystem, depriving 1,500 species of fish of a home in its colourful depths.

Daniel New, Australia

Questions and activities

1. Explain the idea of 'positive feedback' and how it can contribute to global warming.

2. Which countries does the Amazon Rainforest run through?

3. Daniel worries about the Great Barrier Reef. What else could be lost in a globally warmed ocean?

who suffers?

Extreme weather, food and water shortages and species loss are likely to be a feature of all our lives. But, if we look deeper, we find people and animals in the poorest countries will be affected most. And they are the ones least able to protect themselves.

⬆ Flooding is already a major problem in many parts of Asia.

High tides

Global warming does not spell good news for the 2.75 billion people living within 100 km of the world's coastlines. The rate of melting from ice sheets and glaciers is already endangering the survival of low-lying island states like the Maldives. While the Arctic is quickly vanishing, Greenland's glaciers and the colossal ice sheets of Antarctica are now beginning to respond to warmer temperatures. Three degrees of global warming would eventually melt these giant masses of ice enough to raise sea levels by several metres.

Poorer countries such as Bangladesh and the Maldives have few defences to protect themselves from severe and regular flooding. Only wealthy coastal cities such as New York and London might be able to save themselves with extraordinary flood-prevention measures.

Looming famine

The warmer global temperatures get, the harder it will be for us to feed ourselves. Exceeding just 1°C of global warming may see jumps in agricultural output across well-watered northern regions, but many of the poorest nations will see their food production decline. The reason: global warming makes droughts and heat waves – the big crop killers – more likely in areas already most affected.

Central America and 29 African countries are most at risk. Global temperatures rising beyond 2°C could impact Asian food production by making the summer monsoons less reliable – leaving crops to die of thirst one year, and drowning them the next. Food crisis in a world 2°C warmer should be avoidable, but above 3°C starvation would threaten the majority of the world's population.

Thirsty lands

Water shortages could become an issue for several regions in a warmer world. Peru's capital, Lima, depends on natural meltwater from the glaciers of the surrounding mountains to supply its four million inhabitants with water. The chances of these glaciers surviving a 2° rise in global temperatures are slim.

The Himalayan and the Karakoram mountain ranges have some of the world's highest mountains, whose glaciers hold an enormous store of fresh water. Asia's key rivers – the Indus, Ganges, Brahmaputra, Mekong, Yangtze and Yellow River – sustain half of the world's population and depend on meltwater from these glaciers for the bulk of their flow. In a world just 3°C warmer, these glaciers will begin to recede, causing serious water shortages across Asia, especially in Pakistan.

Mass extinction

Human actions unrelated to climate change, like over-fishing and habitat destruction, are already causing the sixth mass extinction of life on Earth – the fifth referring to the disappearance of dinosaurs. At 3°C of warming, up to half the plant and animal species now alive could be extinct. As the Arctic melts, polar bears and ringed seals will be unable to survive; warmer and more acidic oceans will wipe out many species of marine life; the loss of ecosystems in areas like the Amazon and Australia's Wet Tropics, will lead inevitably to the extinction of a wide range of biodiversity.

Meet Issac

An extended period of drought is causing food shortages in Kenya. Kitale, our 'bread basket', has been hit more severely than ever. In 2004, 2006 and 2009, a state of emergency was declared as millions faced malnutrition or even starvation. Cattle are dying from lack of water and grasslands. Thirsty elephants have been found desperately digging for water in dried up river beds. Climate change is making Kenya wait for rain.

Issac Musyoka, Kenya

Questions and activities

1. How do you feel when you read the stories above? Shocked? Angry? Helpless? Determined to do something?

2. What other actions, unrelated to climate change, do you think have caused species extinction?

ho's responsible?

Dangerous global warming is staring us in the face, yet global carbon emissions are skyrocketing. Who is responsible? Those who suffer least from global warming. Those who suffer most are the ones with the lowest carbon emissions.

Rising emissions

Instead of dramatically reducing our CO_2 emissions to prevent the worst consequences of global warming, they have accelerated at a rapid rate – increasing by about 25 per cent between 2000 and 2008. Developed economies, or wealthy nations, account for just one-sixth of the world's population and are responsible for seven out of every 10 tonnes of CO_2 emitted over the last 200 years, making them by far the most responsible for global warming. However, the most recent increases in CO_2 emissions have mostly come from developing nations.

Asia booming

Developing an economy requires investment in energy to fuel growing industries and transport networks, which in today's world means burning oil in vehicles, and coal and gas in power stations. With a combined population of 2.5 billion people, China and India are two rapidly developing economies. In 2006, China overtook the USA as the biggest emitter of CO_2, pumping out 6.2 billion tonnes that year. Even more recently, India has overtaken Japan as the fourth largest emitter from fossil fuels, racking up over one billion tonnes of CO_2 in a year. On current trends, big jumps in coal, oil and gas demand are expected over the next 20 years, and the vast majority of this increase will come from China and India.

World War III

A war has been fought, between progress and preservation.

We feed coal and oil to our mechanized foes. Killers we built, our tools, in our homes.

Among us, we trust them, they move unseen. Murder each one of us in our sleep.

A resistance is rising, a new dawn to our night. A call to arms of a planet, a war cry for life.

A world is being built on progress and preservation.

Mikhail Jordaan, South Africa

Emissions per capita

China and India may now be amongst the biggest CO_2 emitters, but their average citizen has a relatively low carbon footprint. Divide a nation's yearly CO_2 emissions by its population and you get the average carbon footprint per person living

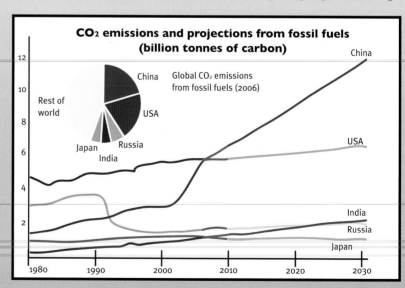

CO_2 emissions and projections from fossil fuels (billion tonnes of carbon)

Global CO_2 emissions from fossil fuels (2006)

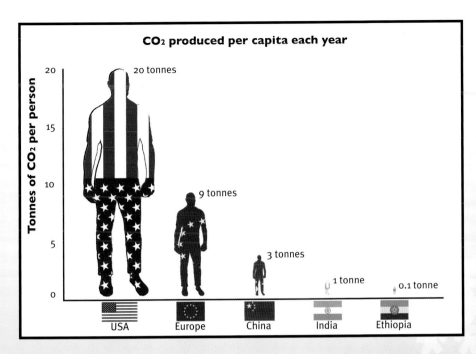

CO₂ produced per capita each year

Tonnes of CO₂ per person

- 20 tonnes — USA
- 9 tonnes — Europe
- 3 tonnes — China
- 1 tonne — India
- 0.1 tonne — Ethiopia

Pakistan, Nigeria, Bangladesh and Indonesia – are likely to account for half of this increase. Not only will it be harder to satisfy the hunger, thirst and other material needs of a greater population, but it will also become even more difficult to limit global CO₂ emissions, as demands for energy and forest clearance for farmland sharply rises.

in the nation for that year (emissions per capita). When the story is told in this way, we find an interesting breakdown of CO₂ emissions.

Population

From 1970 to 2009, the global population almost doubled from 3.7 billion to 6.7 billion, making population growth an important contributory factor to rapidly increasing CO₂ emissions. By 2044, roughly nine billion people are expected to inhabit planet Earth – a population rise of 2.3 billion from 2009. Six countries – India, China,

Worst affected, least responsible

As we identified at the beginning of this chapter, it is the poorest nations that stand to be worst affected by the hardships of climate change. Now, we can clearly see that the poorest people have the smallest carbon footprint, and are therefore the least responsible for climate change. This brings up serious issues of 'climate justice'. Should the developed world take responsibility for climate change? Can developing nations be expected to reduce their emissions? What's fair? We are now going to look at these difficult questions.

Did you know?

When deforestation is taken into account, Indonesia and Brazil emit more CO₂ than India, Russia and Japan.

Questions and activities

1. In what ways do you think population growth affects greenhouse-gas emissions?

2. What does the poet of 'World War III' mean by 'progress and preservation'? Is his poem positive or negative?

'Climate justice'

To help us understand the concept of climate justice, our research team met with Eliot Whittington, policy adviser on climate change for the international development charity Christian Aid.

Why is the developing world particularly affected by climate change?

Climate change is making the lives of many poor people unsustainable *now*, and things are getting worse. Global warming makes the harsh climates of the developing world even harsher. Furthermore, many in the developing world lack access to adequate housing, health care or emergency services. So they are extremely vulnerable to the effects of climate disruptions.

Are people in developing nations concerned about climate change?

Those who recognise that the climate is changing and affecting their livelihoods are, of course, concerned. But they are much more preoccupied with getting out of poverty. While wealthier nations are becoming more worried about a climate-change crisis, half of the world's population is already in a poverty crisis, struggling for daily survival.

Can both poverty and climate change be addressed?

Christian Aid believes that every nation has the right to develop its economy and pull itself out of poverty. And this could be done without accelerating climate change if developing nations had alternative means of growing their economies – other than by burning coal for electricity and clearing their forests for farmland.

Can you suggest a solution?

At Christian Aid, we advocate a model of climate justice, called 'Greenhouse Development Rights'. On this model, each nation is allocated a certain degree of obligation to deal with climate change, based on their economic and technological capacity and their historical responsibility for causing the problem.

What are the 'obligations'?

Developed nations have the greatest capacity and responsibility to tackle climate change. They can help poorer nations skip the 'fossil-fuel' stage of development and move directly to renewable

Did you know?

According to the Global Humanitarian Forum:
- 300,000 deaths a year are directly linked to climate change; this figure could rise to 500,000 by 2030.
- Over the last 30 years, the number of people suffering from climate events each year has doubled to 260 million.
- 98 per cent of those affected by climate change today live in the developing world.
- Over US$110 billion is lost each year in the developing world due to climate change – more than current development aid.

➡ 'Global warming makes the harsh climates of the developing world even harsher.'
Eliot Whittington

energies, like wind and solar. Such large-scale technology transfer could cost the developed world around US$150 billion a year. When shared between dozens of wealthy nations, it's a fairly small sum to help save the planet from climate change, while reducing poverty.

Do developing nations have the responsibility of curbing their emissions and their population growth?

They should do everything they can to develop in a low-carbon way – our planet depends on that. And population growth is an issue – there are already too many of us consuming too many of the Earth's resources. However, when you consider that the average East African emits 200 times less CO_2 than the average citizen in the USA, curbing population growth doesn't seem like the most important or even the most realistic way of tackling climate change.

What *is* the most realistic way of tackling climate change?

The only way that I can see is to build a worldwide post-carbon economy, in which developing nations can grow with minimum carbon emissions and developed nations change their entire way of life to one that is independent of fossil fuels. This would be a massive task, requiring international co-operation, solidarity and investment on a scale not seen since World War II.

Questions and activities

1. List what you think should be developing countries' 'Greenhouse Development Rights'.

2. What could be causing the 300,000 deaths linked to climate change? How might they be saved?

solution: a post-carbon future

a new world by 2050

What is the post-carbon future? It is an energy revolution with social and economic consequences that will transform our world. We know what needs to be done; we know how to do it – and we have to do it to save ourselves from catastrophic climate change.

A new industrial revolution

We have seen one possible future: one where we fail to act, allowing global warming to go beyond 2°C and spiral out of control. But we are not yet locked into this future – there is still time to make the choice for a better world. It's a world where we end our addiction to fossil fuels and kick our CO_2 habit. We call it the post-carbon future.

Reaching for a post-carbon future means rethinking how we run society: it means new transport systems; a new wave of low-carbon technologies and fuels; a new way of getting electricity and heat; a new way of constructing our homes and other buildings; and a new way of living. Ultimately, it would be a worldwide industrial and social revolution. And it all needs to happen in your lifetime!

What needs to be done?

Limiting global warming to 2°C means that the CO_2 budget for this century should be 14 billion tonnes per year. Currently, emissions are running at twice this level and as economies continue to develop and world population explodes, demand for energy is soaring. At this rate, we could be emitting 62 billion tonnes of CO_2 a year by 2050. This would easily take the planet to 3°C of warming. The real challenge for the post-carbon future is to cater for a doubling in global energy demand while cutting at least 80 per cent of CO_2 emissions compared to 1990 levels – all by 2050.

How are we going to do it?

Reducing the amount of energy that buildings, industries and vehicles consume by making them operate more efficiently is one crucial way of making deep cuts in CO_2 emissions. Another key strategy is to ensure that the energy consumed comes from clean forms of energy generation, like solar, wind and geothermal – not fossil fuels. Below is a realistic summary, suggesting the contribution that energy-efficient measures and alternative means of power generation could make to meeting projected energy demand in 2050, while achieving 80 per cent in emissions cuts.

A post-carbon pie for 2050

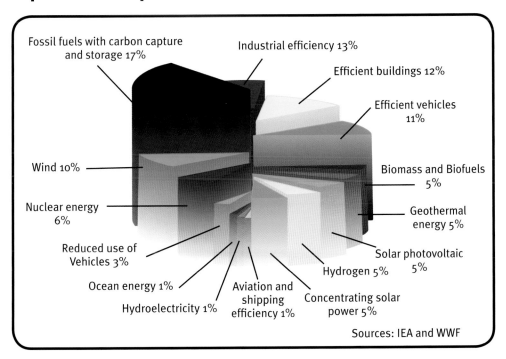

Fossil fuels with carbon capture and storage 17%
Industrial efficiency 13%
Efficient buildings 12%
Efficient vehicles 11%
Wind 10%
Biomass and Biofuels 5%
Nuclear energy 6%
Geothermal energy 5%
Reduced use of Vehicles 3%
Solar photovoltaic 5%
Ocean energy 1%
Aviation and shipping efficiency 1%
Concentrating solar power 5%
Hydrogen 5%
Hydroelectricity 1%

Sources: IEA and WWF

How much?

Miika Tomiila from the International Energy Agency (IEA) told our research team that 'The post-carbon future would cost the world about $45 trillion to build.' This may seem like a big figure, but Tomiila notes that it's really not that much: 'Spread over 40 years, it amounts to only 1 per cent of the world's wealth.' He goes on to point out that 'The costs of dealing with the consequences of climate change later would be much greater than the costs of preventing it now.'

No need to wait

Building the post-carbon future may seem like a tall order, but it can be done. According to Professor Ralph Simms from the IEA: 'The technologies and strategies to do it are there now and ready to be exploited – we don't have to wait.' In the pages that follow, we want to explore what the post-carbon future could look like and what we can do to make it happen. We have the technology, the finances and just enough time, so, what are we waiting for?

post-carbon power

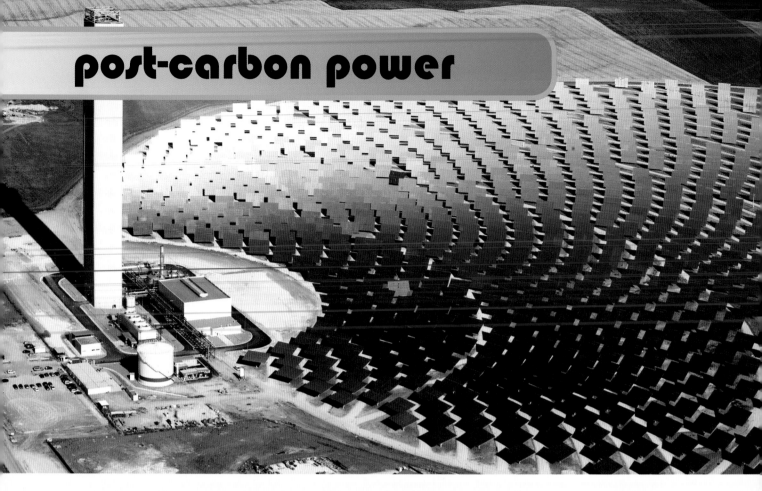

In just six hours, deserts lap up more energy from the sun than humanity consumes in a whole year. But how to harness it? A growing number of experts, investors and politicians are beginning to believe that Concentrating Solar Power (CSP) is the answer. Dr Gerry Wolff from the Desertec Foundation gave our research team the full story.

⬆ Solar power tower: Spain's PS10.

What is Desertec?

Desertec is a growing international organisation operating to promote a big concept: covering less than 1 per cent of the Sahara Desert (or 0.3 per cent of the world's deserts) with CSP technology could provide EUMENA – Europe, the Middle East and North Africa – with the bulk of their electricity needs. The technologies to do this have been around for over 20 years. In operation they emit no CO_2, and the time has come to put them into action on a massive scale, with other renewables.

What are the main technologies?

Solar power towers are a promising CSP technology. They operate with an array of mirrors that concentrate the sun's rays on to a boiler in a tower, heating it to temperatures of about 1,000°C. The heated boiler generates steam, which is driven through turbines to make electricity. Other CSP technologies, like solar troughs, effectively work off a similar principle.

But how will the plant operate at night and on cloudy days?

CSP plants can produce power when there is no sun. Simply using the solar energy collected during the day to heat a vat of molten salt, the plant can continue to operate during the night or on cloudy days, as the heat stored in the salt is released to make steam. If there is a succession of cloudy days, they can temporarily switch to gas.

Okay, but how can the solar power generated in the Sahara Desert find its way to Europe?

Essential to achieving this is a high-voltage transmission grid across EUMENA. With grid technology like this, anywhere within 3,000 km of a CSP plant could be provided with clean power from the desert.

So what's holding the Desertec concept back?

Until recently, there was a general lack of awareness that this kind of project is even possible. But all that changed in July 2009, when major companies, like Deutsche Bank, E.ON and Siemens came together in a US$400 billion project to make the Desertec concept a reality. By 2020, they hope to be supplying Europe with power from the Sahara Desert, eventually meeting 15 per cent of its electricity demand.

Amazing, but is CSP contributing to our power supply today?

The world's newest CSP plants in operation today – PS10 and PS20 – are in Spain's Andalusian desert, near Seville. Both plants are part of the Solucar platform that will see the addition of five further plants by 2013, generating carbon-free power for 600,000 of Seville's citizens. California plans to build anywhere up to nine CSP stations in its desert lands – beginning in 2011 – which will provide over a million homes with electricity.

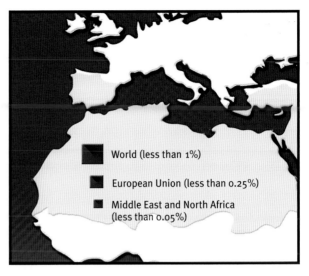

World (less than 1%)

European Union (less than 0.25%)

Middle East and North Africa (less than 0.05%)

⬆ Each red square represents the total amount of land that would need to be covered with CSP technology to supply a given area with electricity. Figures are based on electricity consumption in 2005. (Source: Desertec Foundation)

CSP seems like it can work for EUMENA, but does it have worldwide potential?

CSP technology could meet up to 25 per cent of global energy demand by 2050. It could help provide countries throughout Africa and much of South America with clean power. And in countries heavily dependent on fossil fuels – like the USA, India, Australia and China – CSP could be the key to weaning them off their addiction.

Questions and activities

1. Other than clean electricity, what benefits could building CSP stations in the Middle East and North Africa bring to these areas?

2. You work for the Desertec Foundation. Make up a poster with slogans, images and key facts to get the Desertec concept across.

Our solar future

CSP is just one way of harnessing the sun's energy. We have photovoltaic (PV) panels, too. And the best part is we can use solar PVs almost anywhere. Don't forget, we also have solar water heaters, solar cookers, solar thin film and, soon, solar paint. The possibilities are endless.

Solar boom

Solar photovoltaic (PV) technology is a fancy name for the kind of solar panels we are all familiar with. Sometimes we see them fixed to houses and other buildings, lapping up sunlight and converting it into electricity. One big advantage of solar panels is that they can still produce power on cloudy days, making them practical over a wide range of locations.

Homes in southern Germany have shown how rooftop solar panels can provide all their electricity needs. Apartment blocks, high-rise buildings and factories are producing their own solar power; communities of all sizes – urban and rural – are successfully feeding off PV power plants laid out over large areas of land. The PV industry is now the fastest growing in the world and if things continue, solar panels have the potential to produce 12 per cent of the world's electricity by 2030 – equivalent to 450 coal-fired power plants.

Did you know?

Taiwan has a 50,000-seat stadium whose 3,300 lights and jumbo vision screens are all powered entirely by solar panels.

Thin film

Excitement about a new wave of solar technology has been buzzing for some time. It's called solar thin film and it could be the future of solar PV. The new film is 17 times thinner than a standard solar panel (0.01 mm) and it can be used virtually anywhere. Printed like a newspaper on to a lightweight metal or plastic, as well as going on the top and sides of buildings, the film can be fixed to car roofs, or even stuck on a backpack to charge a phone while you walk.

Solar thin film power plants are in the pipeline in New Mexico and California that will each produce electricity for up to 300,000 homes. Developments in solar technology don't stop with thin film though – plastics, windows and even paint could be generating solar electricity for us in the near future.

⬆ PV solar panels and the 'Sunny Beam', a device used to measure their performance.

Heating up

Solar panels provide clean electricity, but zero-carbon hot water can come from solar water heaters. They consist of glass tubes fixed to a rooftop, which collect the sun's rays to heat water, stored in a tank. Once installed, each unit can provide a family of four with zero-carbon showers. In Israel, 90 per cent of households own one, they have recently been made compulsory for new homes in Hawaii, and they are becoming increasingly popular in China, featured in one-tenth of all houses.

Concentrator solar cooker: sunlight is concentrated on the cooking pot.

Solar cookers

Cooking in rural areas of developing countries is generally done on smoky, inefficient wood-burning stoves that sometimes cause health problems. Many developing countries have sun-blessed climates ideal for using solar cookers, which could provide families with cheap, carbon-free meals.

By reducing the need to burn wood for fuel, solar cookers could improve people's health in the developing world, while helping to combat deforestation. Concentrator cookers are one common type of solar cooker and are most widely used in China.

Questions and activities

1. There are CSP and PV power plants. List what you think might be the advantages of each.

2. You are a town/city planner asked to make maximum use of solar thin film and solar water heaters in your town/city. Where would you decide to put them?

Harvesting the wind, tapping the heat

Wind farms continue to dot the globe, leading the way to the post-carbon future. Meanwhile, heat from the ground is increasingly being exploited to supply zero-carbon electricity, indoor heating and hot water.

Asian wind

The Indian company Suzlon is one of the world's largest wind-turbine manufacturers, led by self-made billionaire Tulsi Tanti. 'Our country needs power for its economic growth, and clean, green power is the best option,' he says. With this in mind, by 2010 Suzlon will complete the world's largest wind farm in Dhule, India, with a capacity of 1,000 MW – equivalent to one nuclear power plant. This greatly surpasses the 735 MW capacity of the Horse Hollow Wind Energy Centre in Texas. Tanti won't stop there, either, as he plans to move on to even bigger projects in China, which has announced its intention to get 10 per cent of its power from wind by 2020 (100,000 MW). This would make China the world leader in wind energy installations.

Did you know?

The amount of electricity the world gets from wind power is set to quadruple by 2017.

Offshore wind

Many of the best spots for generating wind energy have been taken up on European land, so now farms are being planned up to 100 km out at sea where the breeze is much stronger. Offshore wind alone could provide the UK with all its electricity needs, so the potential for development is great. In Europe, more than 30,000 MW of offshore wind energy is planned for completion by 2015. Within this time frame, England hopes to take up 232 sq km of its east coast with the world's biggest offshore wind farm – 1,000 MW – which will power up to 500,000 homes. Tom Dealy, of the CO_2 reduction company the Carbon Trust, estimates that 'by 2020 the UK could represent almost half of the global market for offshore wind power.'

◄ Offshore wind in Demark. Spot the kayakers for scale.

⬆ Bathers enjoy Iceland's Blue Lagoon hot springs, as the power plant taps the geothermal heat below to produce steam.

water thousands of metres underground to be heated by hot rocks. It is then shot back up as steam, which can be used by a power plant to drive turbines to make zero-carbon electricity. Once cooled, the water can be piped to buildings for indoor heating and hot water.

The USA, the Philippines, Indonesia and Mexico already use large amounts of geothermal energy. The USA could get 10 per cent of its electricity from geothermal by 2025, while geothermal power from Cornwall could supply one-tenth of the UK's electricity.

Meet Katla

Icelanders have been using geothermal heat for 1,200 years. We have always enjoyed hot springs for bathing and relaxation. Nowadays, 20 per cent of our electricity and 90 per cent of our indoor heating and hot water comes from geothermal sources. If all the geothermal sites were exploited on our small volcanic island, it would probably be enough to satisfy the electricity demand of the entire Northern Hemisphere.

Katla Björg Kristjánsdóttir, Iceland

Earth heat

Just as we can harness energy from the sun and the wind, so too will the Earth's heat be a part of the post-carbon future. It's called geothermal energy and it's already a big renewable resource in some places. Exploiting geothermal energy often means installing a plumbing system that pumps

Pumping heat

A ground source or air source heat pump could be installed in every new home. This works like a refrigerator in reverse, drawing small amounts of heat from the air, or from pipes underground, and compressing it to heat up water or air. Such pumps can reduce carbon emissions by 70 per cent. And, during summer, the pumps can extract warm air from the building to cool it.

Questions and activities

1. What might be the advantages and disadvantages of onshore and offshore wind energy? Would you object to a wind farm being built near your home? Why/why not?

2. Write a letter to the people of Cornwall in the UK, explaining the advantages of getting geothermal electricity.

Go with the flow!

Our rivers and oceans never stop moving, and this makes them an incredible source of renewable energy. Rivers have generated power for centuries – sometimes controversially. Oceans and tides are energy giants, waiting to be harnessed.

River power

Brazil, Norway, Iceland and the Democratic Republic of the Congo receive more than 80 per cent of their electricity from hydroelectric power plants, which use the energy of flowing rivers to turn turbines and produce electricity. While many parts of the developed world have already exploited their hydro resources, the developing world is expanding on its hydroelectric projects.

Almost 26,000 large dams exist in China alone and there are plans for many more. When the final touches are completed in 2011, the Three Gorges Dam will be the world's biggest, capable of producing more electricity than 22 nuclear power plants combined. Meanwhile, several hundred dams are planned or under construction on rivers flowing out of the Himalayas, eventually providing India, Pakistan, Nepal and Bhutan with vast quantities of electricity.

Hydro impact

While hydroelectric power stations have been providing the world with clean energy for decades, critics urge caution in rapid hydroelectric expansion. According to the environmental charity International Rivers, 'Around the world large dams are causing social and environmental devastation.' The Three Gorges Dam, for instance, it calls 'a model for disaster'. Already it has displaced more than a million people, caused landslides, water pollution and floods. International Rivers is campaigning across the developing world for fewer and better dams to be built.

Small and micro hydro

Small-scale hydro installations tend to have few negative impacts on the environment and can provide entire communities in the developing world with power. The World Bank is especially enthusiastic in supporting these projects, estimating that up to 70 per cent of global potential for small hydro remains untapped. Even micro-hydro systems are available, which can cater for the power demands of homes sitting near rivers or streams.

⬆ The Three Gorges Dam is 185 m high and 2.3 km long.

Ocean technology

According to Professor Ralph Simms from the IEA, 'Most ocean energy technologies are in the same stage of development as wind energy was about 30 years ago, when things kept breaking.' With persistence though, he believes we can harness great amounts of energy from ocean waves and tides. Here are just some of the ocean technologies likely to play a part in the post-carbon future.

Tidal turbines

Tidal power turbines work just like normal wind turbines, except instead of wind they are driven by incoming and withdrawing underwater currents. The only operating tidal turbine in existence lies in Irish waters. This technology, however, is ready for use on a massive scale and by 2015 it will be powering 150,000 South Korean homes.

Pelamis

Since 2006, the Pelamis project has been operating in Northern Portugal. Three flexible hydraulic 'sea-snakes', each 140 m long, bob up and down on the waves to drive electricity generators that produce enough power for 1,000 homes. The sea-snakes have broken down on occasion, but if the technology proves to be reliable and cost effective after further development, it could be coming to a shoreline near you.

Barrage power

The tidal barrage works on a similar principle to hydroelectric dams, using incoming and outgoing tides to turn turbines. La Rance, off the east coast of France, is the only barrage of note, providing 200,000 homes with electricity since the 1960s. Tidal barrages across the Severn Estuary in the UK have been proposed and could meet 5 per cent of the UK's energy demands. Canada's Bay of Fundy and the mouth of China's Yalu River could also boast large barrages in the post-carbon future.

Questions and activities

1. A hydroelectric dam is proposed for a nearby river. Write a letter to a local politician explaining why you are for or against the project.

2. Explain the difference between harnessing the power of tides and harnessing the power of waves.

Super-smart distribution

Existing AC electricity grids allow the transmission of electricity distances of 400–500 km. Ultra-high voltage DC grids allow transmission 10 times that distance. Also, a new kind of Internet will create super-smart grids that turn a country into a virtual power station.

Super-grid to the rescue

One major problem plaguing many renewable technologies is their variability. Solar power generation depends on the strength of the sun and is only available in daylight. Wind power is reliant on wind speeds. In other words, sometimes renewable technologies produce too much energy and at other times they produce too little. Fred Pearce, environmental consultant for *New Scientist* magazine, believes that a 'super-grid' could solve this problem 'and be the missing link to turn renewables from being a fairly minor source of energy to the powerhouse of Europe.'

EUMENA Super-grid

Linking up

A European super-grid would link up renewable energy projects to deliver the right amount of power to the right place at the right time. If Portugal's solar installations are suffering from cloud cover, for instance, it could tap wind power from Spain or France. Likewise, when Portugal's solar plants are producing excess power, they will be able to sell it to other parts of the world.

Some super-grid links are already in place: when the wind dies down in Denmark, for example, it buys hydroelectricity from Norway. The EUMENA project to supply Europe with solar power from the Sahara by 2020 would add more super-grid links.

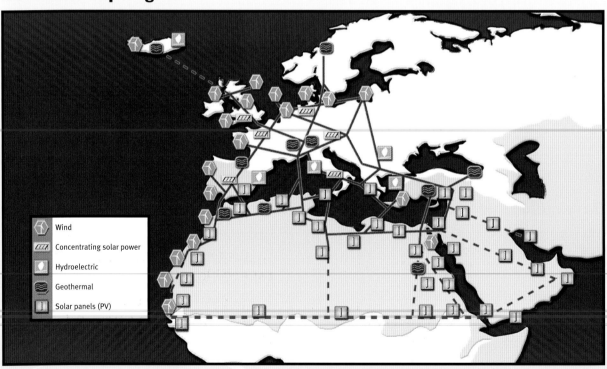

Wind

Concentrating solar power

Hydroelectric

Geothermal

Solar panels (PV)

⬆ The super-grid as it might look, spanning EUMENA. Through ultra-high voltage underground transmission lines, power moves from one part of the world to another as it is needed. (Source: Desertec Foundation)

Smart electricity

The national power grids now in operation carry only electricity. For the post-carbon future, they need smartening up so they can transmit information as well. A smart-grid would link an electricity meter on your wall to a whole network that calculates how much power is needed and when – adapting the electricity-generating capacity to fit. It will also use this information to explain how homes and offices can reduce their energy needs. It will know if offices leave their lights on at night and suggest the installation of motion-sensor systems.

Smart grids will become essential as more homes and buildings produce their own electricity with solar panels, small wind turbines and other renewable technologies. Already, the German government has introduced incentives along with smart meters to make it easy and profitable for private buildings to produce their own power with renewables and sell to the grid any electricity they don't use. A smart-grid would make this system much more efficient – regulating the relation-ship between the grid, normal power plants and ordinary people who produce their own energy.

Super smart

Energy experts dream that super-smart grids will span continents in the post-carbon future. Such a network would minimise energy waste by intelligently co-ordinating all the different energy sources – from solar panels on your roof to massive wind farms in Spain – with the constantly fluctuating energy demands of all the buildings in the different countries supplied by this grid. As smart-grid technology develops and decision-makers begin to talk more about building high-voltage DC grids, super-smart grids could be just decades away.

Did you know?

In preparation for a smart grid, 40 million homes in the USA will be fitted with a smart meter by 2012, and every home in the UK is expected to have one by 2020.

Questions and activities

1. Why does Fred Pearce think the super-grid is the 'missing-link' for renewable energy?

2. Make a poster that explains the idea of a super-smart grid and what it would contribute to the post-carbon future.

Coal habits die hard

Coal is the dirtiest fossil fuel. It generates 40 per cent of the world's electricity – much more in some countries where its use is an economic imperative. Could carbon capture and storage (CCS) help us use coal safely, or should we leave it underground?

Big coal consumers								
Country	South Africa	Poland	Australia	China	India	Germany	USA	UK
Electricity from coal	90%	90%	85%	70%	70%	50%	50%	30%

What is carbon capture and storage?

Excitement about CCS stems from the fact that it could cut emissions from coal-fired power plants by up to 90 per cent. A process called 'scrubbing' chemically separates carbon from the coal before or after it is burned. The captured CO_2 is then compressed into liquid form and pumped down pipelines to storage sites located deep underground or under the sea.

Support for CCS

Miika Tomiila from the IEA told our research team that CCS is a safe technology and that the likelihood of CO_2 leaking from its storage sites is minimal. 'CCS is a route that must be explored if countries refuse to stop burning coal,' he says. The United Nations, WWF and many governments echo this view. With such support, CCS looks set play a big role in the post-carbon future.

Did you know?

Every week a new coal-fired power plant is completed in China.

CARBON CAPTURE AND STORAGE DEBATE

We need all the help we can get to cut emissions, while meeting the growing energy demand. Coal with CCS must be part of the post-carbon energy mix.

Coal reserves should be able to meet increasing demand for the next 200 years. CCS will let us use this precious resource safely.

FOR

Coal in the hole

'Keep the coal in the hole!' This is the cry of climate activist groups like Leave it in the Ground and The Coal Hole. They believe that simply refusing to build more coal-fired power stations, while gradually replacing old ones with renewable energy, is the best way to address our climate woes. But nations with a well-established coal industry are reluctant to give up this cheap source of energy in favour of building an expensive post-carbon energy infrastructure. Instead of closing down coal-fired power stations, new ones are going up across the world.

Did you know?

Once built, a coal-fired power station has a life span of up to 75 years.

CCS is still in development. It is likely to be many years before it is widely used. With CO_2 emissions rising fast, CCS may be too little too late.

Installing CCS will be easiest on new power plants near places where CO_2 can be buried. It will be hard to fit CCS to existing ones.

AGAINST

Meet David

I am one of many campaigning against coal-fired power stations, like the one proposed for Kingsnorth in the UK. Pumping billions of dollars into CCS technology will draw investment away from renewable energy, which is the only long-term solution because coal will eventually run out. While CCS is an unproven technology, we are going to have to imagine a society that is not powered by coal, and work towards it.

David Cullen, UK

Questions and activities

1. Think of one more argument for each side of the debate.

2. Write a letter to your local politician, explaining why they should or shouldn't support CCS as part of our energy future.

3. Why do you think countries continue burning coal, in spite of its damage to the environment?

4. Do you agree with David Cullen's point of view? Write a response.

The nuclear question

Radioactive dumping scandals, the Chernobyl nuclear disaster, links to nuclear weapons programmes in Iran and North Korea – all of this has given nuclear power a bad reputation. But it is a low-carbon way of generating electricity. Should it be part of our post-carbon future? Opinion is hotly divided.

Anti-nuclear

The UN refuses to call nuclear power 'sustainable'. Greenpeace, Friends of the Earth, the US Natural Resources Defence Council and most environmental groups are opposed to nuclear. WWF argues: 'Nuclear power is not a sustainable source of energy. The entire commercial process of nuclear mining, processing uranium ore, operating nuclear power stations, handling and re-processing nuclear waste is full of leaks that leaves a highly toxic legacy for hundreds of thousands of years… Replacing fossil fuel-fired power stations with nuclear energy simply replaces one fundamental environmental problem with another.'

Environmentalists from the anti-nuclear camp believe that we don't actually need nuclear power. Major investment in renewable energy and technologies like super- and smart-grids, they say, should be more than enough to meet future low-carbon energy demand. Economists point out that nuclear power historically has required huge government subsidies, if only to deal with the expenses associated with nuclear waste disposal. Renewables may well be the low-cost option.

Did you know?

With over 440 power plants in operation today, nuclear energy supplies 16 per cent of the world's electricity.

> Only nuclear power has the capacity to provide energy in the volumes that the world needs now and in the future. Nuclear science is in its infancy: it can only get better and safer!

> Compared to the coal industry, where thousands of miners die each year, nuclear is a far safer option. Save lives, go nuclear!

Pro-nuclear

Nuclear power stations may produce radioactive waste, but they emit hardly any CO_2. Respected environmentalist and scientist James Lovelock writes: 'I entreat my fellow Greens to drop their wrongheaded objection to nuclear energy. Even if they were right about its dangers, and they're not, its worldwide use as our main source of energy would pose an insignificant threat compared with the dangers of lethal heat waves and sea levels rising to drown every coastal city of the world.'

Indeed, Professor Ralph Simms from the IEA assures us that 'nuclear power plants are far safer than they were in the past, reducing a small risk even further.'

Fast-breeders

Mark Lynas believes that a new generation of even safer 'fast-breeder' nuclear power plants could address some of the anti-nuclear concerns. These power plants, not yet developed, should be sixty times more efficient because they actually use what would be toxic waste in today's power plants as fuel to make energy. Any waste they do produce would be minimal and unfit for use in nuclear weapons programmes.

By 2021, Germany will have shut down all its nuclear power plants. They know they don't need it: they can get all the power they need from safe, renewable sources. All of us can!

Nuclear waste is a deadly gift to pass on to future generations. Power plants and storage sites are massively dangerous terrorist targets. Our children will never forgive us if we go for nuclear power without having tried every possible alternative.

Debate for the planet

Some love it,
it will save us from global warming.
Others hate it,
fearing radioactive waste.
O sublime blue planet,
what do you think of it all?
You who are the centre of the debate.
You who offer us glorious treasures,
without shadow or toxic cloud.

Fatiha Fekih, France

Questions and activities

1. Think of one more argument that each side could make.

2. Why do you think Germany is shutting down its nuclear power programme when other nations are eager to expand on theirs?

3. Write a poem expressing your views about nuclear power.

transport revolution

What will be the fuels of the future, powering our cars, planes, ships and trains? Hydrogen, biofuels and electricity are the key, low-carbon contenders to replace oil. And we need to act fast: dangerous climate change is upon us and oil is quickly running out.

Peak oil

Transport accounts for 16 per cent of global CO_2 emissions, which means that we need to revolutionise our transport sector to effectively tackle climate change. Oil burnt in our cars, trucks, planes and ships is the primary culprit for these emissions. However, the global economy relies on these oil-based transport systems to move people and goods around, so we can't just stop using oil without causing chaos.

This chaos is unavoidable, however, if we hit peak oil. This means that the amount of oil we are able to discover and extract will eventually reach its maximum, or peak, and then begin to run out – possibly within the next thirty years. To avoid the double crunch of climate change and peak oil, we need to replace oil with fuels and technologies that have low-carbon emissions. Let's take a look at some of the post-carbon fuels on offer.

Hydrogen

Hydrogen is one of the cleanest fuels known to man. When burnt, nothing but water vapour is produced. Hydrogen can be made from gas and coal, but the most non-polluting way is by simply passing an electric current through water – a process called electrolysis. Hydrogen is a completely zero-carbon fuel, if the electricity used to make it comes from renewable energy.

Unfortunately, it takes much more energy to create the hydrogen than the hydrogen itself gives out when burned, making it a very inefficient fuel. Nevertheless, massive investment is going into hydrogen to ensure that it is a major player in the post-carbon future. The hydrogen 'fuel cell' is key to making this happen. It operates like an electric battery, except it uses hydrogen gas for fuel.

Biofuels

We can use crops and other organic matter as raw materials to make fuel, or biofuel, fit for standard vehicles. Overall, biofuels are considered to have no carbon emissions – the crops absorb CO_2 to grow, they are then harvested for oil, burned in vehicles and released as CO_2, which is absorbed by the next crop. The first generation of biofuels was made from food crops and had disastrous consequences. In 2008, the World Bank announced that the race to use food for fuel had caused serious food shortages in the developing world, pushing another 100 million people below the poverty line.

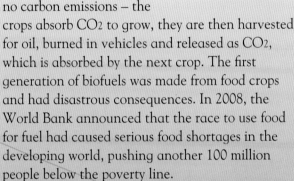

This failure has encouraged the development of a second generation of biofuels, made from non-food crops. Although they may not directly impact food supplies, environmentalists worry that this new generation would lead to forests being cleared for biofuel crops, which would do anything but save carbon emissions. With strict regulation, the European Union, amongst others, aims to ensure that all its biofuels are sustainably sourced.

Algae

The third generation of biofuel is made from algae. That's right – the green sludge that coats ponds can be used instead of oil. Algae grow quickly, doubling in weight several times a day and absorbing large quantities of CO_2 in the process.

Growing in controlled glass tanks or artificial ponds, it makes little demand on land. Still in the development stage, algae biofuel isn't yet readily available, but experts believe that it could be seriously competing as a post-carbon fuel by 2020.

Low-carbon electricity

Electricity already has a place in the transport sector, running our trains and trams. In the post-carbon future, it could also drive most cars, trucks and agricultural machinery too. But, it's vital that the electricity powering them comes from low-carbon sources, such as wind and solar. Electricity drawn from normal coal-fired power stations perpetuates the problem.

Questions and activities

1. Why is peak oil an important issue? If oil began to run out today, what would be the consequences for your area and the world at large?

2. Make a poster to raise awareness about the different fuels that we could use to power the post-carbon transport system.

Plug in to a better place

Could electric cars be the choice for a post-carbon future? Entrepreneur Shai Agassi thinks so. He's on a mission to end our addiction to oil with a plug, a battery and a robotic arm.

Starting early

Shai Agassi made his first business deal at 14 years old, promising his father 10 per cent of his lifetime profits from writing software if only he bought him a computer. And what a deal it was. Agassi founded a software company at 21 and sold it for over $450 million nine years later. Now, he is on a mission to end dependence on oil. Squarely focused on this task, he has set up Better Place, a company dedicated to ensuring that the electric vehicle becomes the future of zero-carbon transport.

Battery problem

'The electric car is becoming inevitable.' This at least is Agassi's view, as he believes Better Place has cracked the major obstacle to the widespread adoption of the electric car – slow and regular battery recharging. Although technology is improving all the time, a typical electric car battery will go for around 160 km on a single charge, and a full charge can take between three and seven hours, depending on the model.

Better solution

Better Place takes a twofold approach to solving the problem of battery recharging.

• Charging points: install plug-in charging points where cars spend most of their time – in homes, on streets, outside work places and in car parks.

• Battery switching: set up a network of battery-switching stations for drivers who want to travel long distances. Simply pulling into the station, a robotic arm can replace the wasted battery with a fresh one in less than a minute.

Agassi already has the go-ahead to build these Better Place networks of charging points and

⬆ Shai Agassi charging up.

How battery-charging stations work

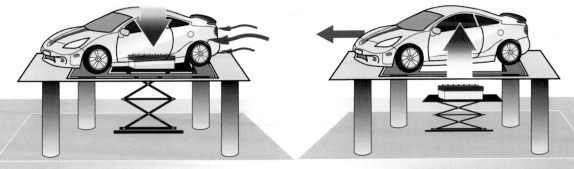

1. Car drives over pit

2. Robotic arm removes battery

3. Robotic arm inserts new battery

4. Car leaves one minute after arriving

battery-switching stations (an 'Electric Recharge Grid') in Israel, Denmark, Japan, Australia, California, Hawaii and Canada. By 2015, he plans to have at least 40 million electric cars on the road working within Electric Recharge Grids. A high priority for Agassi is ensuring that renewable resources – not coal – power electric cars. In Israel, for instance, a solar-powered Recharge Grid is being specially constructed and wind power will be used in Denmark.

Smart driving

An onboard computer, rather like a satellite navigation system, will have a key role to play in Agassi's Better Place system. The computer would be linked to the Electric Recharge Grid, providing the driver with information on available charging points when approaching a destination, or else the nearest switching stations if the battery cannot make the full journey.

Worldwide ambition

Because China plays such a huge role in the global economy, Agassi sees it as the key to worldwide adoption of the electric car. 'Once China does it,' he says, 'you don't have a choice.' Although

nothing like a Better Place Electric Recharge Grid has been proposed in China, Agassi believes that it is on the verge of embracing the electric car as the government and Chinese manufacturers show growing interest.

Electricity versus hydrogen

Agassi has chosen to champion electric instead of hydrogen cars, mainly because it takes far less electricity to charge them than it does to produce hydrogen, and an infrastructure for electric cars is easier to put in place. Indeed, most manufacturers are forging ahead with producing electric cars and hybrid-electric vehicles, but few have given up on hydrogen. What kind of low-carbon car you will be driving in the coming years is anyone's guess.

Questions and activities

1. What do you see as the key breakthroughs in Shai Agassi's plan for introducing electric cars?

2. What could prevent the global introduction of Better Place electric car networks?

low-carbon cars

The age of the private car is far from over. But the age of the low-carbon car is just beginning. Shai Agassi may be pushing electric vehicles, but it's not the only way of cutting CO2 emissions and oil consumption. What are the other options?

Two problems with hydrogen

The Japanese government alone wants to see five million hydrogen vehicles on its roads by 2020 and there is significant investment going into developing the hydrogen car across Europe and the USA. But bringing the hydrogen car into the mainstream runs into two big problems.

• A hydrogen car, with a fully fuelled tank the same size as a standard petrol tank, wouldn't be able to travel nearly as far as the petrol car.

• Although highways with hydrogen refuelling stations exist in Norway, Canada, Japan and California, there aren't yet enough hydrogen vehicles to economically set up a large network of these stations. And few people will buy a hydrogen car unless this infrastructure exists. Does the chicken or the egg come first?

A hydrogen future?

Although hydrogen vehicles may become generally available to the public by 2020, many experts believe that the problems associated with the hydrogen car will stop it becoming a significant piece in the post-carbon puzzle for at least another 40 years. 'We don't have the time,' says energy expert Dr Joseph Romm. Such critics are enthusiastic about the long-term future of the hydrogen car, but say we should be focusing on solutions that can more immediately reduce CO2 emissions on a large scale. This includes measures to ensure vast improvements in fuel efficiency and the development of the electric car.

An alternative model

One UK company, Riversimple, is holding out hopes that its light, two-seater hydrogen car will bring about a hydrogen revolution sooner than expected. Unveiled in 2009, the prototype

Did you know?

600 million cars are on the roads today. That figure could triple by 2050 with increasing demand from the developing world.

↑ Riversimple's two-seater hydrogen car.

↑ Volkswagen's two-seater fuel-efficient car can travel 100 km on less than one litre of fuel.

can travel up to 80 km/h and over 320 km per refuelling. Due for production in 2013, Riversimple have even teamed up with a gas company that will set up hydrogen refuelling points in areas where the vehicle is promoted. If uptake is keen, this system could quickly provide the UK with a basic hydrogen infrastructure.

Fuel efficiency

Using less fuel is an important strategy for reducing CO_2 emissions from road travel. Many cars today use more fuel per kilometre than the Model T Ford, which was released in 1908. Why? Because big, fast cars need big engines that consume large amounts of fuel such as diesel or petrol. Beginning to address this problem, the EU has declared that by 2020 all new cars must use less fuel and emit 40 per cent less CO_2 per kilometre, compared to the average European car. Similar measures for 2016 have been adopted in the USA.

Quite a few small, light vehicles, such as the two-seater Smart Car, have already surpassed these targets. Hybrid vehicles – usually consisting of a small, efficient diesel engine and a powerful electric motor – are going even further, with the Toyota Prius emitting almost 45 per cent less CO_2 than the average European car.

Biofuel cars

Increasingly, flexi-fuel cars are coming on the market, which can run on pure petrol/diesel or a mixture of up to 85 per cent second-generation biofuel – usually ethanol made from sugar cane. Flexi-fuel vehicles have taken over in Brazil, with half of its transport sector now powered by biofuels. As the biggest biofuel producer in the world, the USA has around eight million flexi-fuel cars on its roads. Meanwhile the EU aims to have biofuels making up 10 per cent of all transport fuels by 2020.

Questions and activities

1. How do you think fuel efficiency could have a positive impact on global warming and peak oil?

2. Other than produing less CO_2, what do you see as the benefits of low-carbon cars?

3. Would it be a good thing for the world to have two billion cars by 2050? Think of the advantages and disadvantages.

Greener modes of transport

Millions of people around the world, one to each car, head to work every day and then head home again. Traffic jams, stress and massive CO_2 emissions are the end result. New, improved public-transport systems must be a big part of the solution.

Room for improvement

Around three-quarters of global transport emissions come from road travel. According to transport analyst Lynn Sloman, in many developed countries around 40 per cent of car journeys could already be made by bicycle, on foot or using public transport. A further 40 per cent could be made this way if there were improvements in public transport and cycling facilities. She estimates that just 20 per cent of car journeys couldn't be practically replaced with alternative modes of transport.

Integrated transport

European countries such as Switzerland, Austria and the Netherlands are known for having some of the best and most widely used public-transport systems in the world, because they take an integrated approach. What this means is that all different forms of public transport are co-ordinated to make it an easier, swifter and more reliable way to travel than using a car. Nationwide, trains, trams and buses are scheduled to meet one another. They generally have space for bicycles and bicycle lanes that connect with transport networks across entire cities. Adopting similar systems throughout the world would encourage a large proportion of motorists to use public transport, significantly reducing CO_2 emissions from transport.

Journalist and energy expert George Monbiot stresses that it's not enough to simply make public transport more attractive – driving must also be made less attractive. Congestion charges that put a tax on polluting vehicles entering busy parts of a city, for example, are already effective in Milan and London.

If this group took a car each.

If they all went by bus.

If they went by bike.

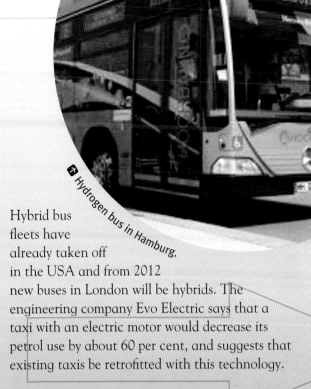
Hydrogen bus in Hamburg.

Meet Santiago

On moving to Barcelona, I discovered 'Bicing' – a cheap system that allows you to borrow one of 5,600 bikes from 375 stations located across the city, just by swiping your membership card. You can then ride to your destination and drop it off at another station, where somebody else can pick it up. It's healthy, it saves time and it's environmentally friendly. Perfect urban transport!

Santiago Thibaud, Argentina

Low-carbon transport

Although public transport is by far the cleanest way to travel, it still tends to produce CO_2. Projects are underway across the world, modelling ways to minimise carbon emissions from public transport. Here is just a small sample.

Hydrogen bus

Hamburg in Germany wants to become a leading city in the economic use of hydrogen. It has begun by deploying six public buses that run on hydrogen fuel cells. This is part of an initiative called HyFLEET:CUTE, concerned with getting a hydrogen-based transport system off the ground. Already, it is testing 33 hydrogen-powered buses in regular public-transport services across nine cities, including London, Beijing and Perth in Australia.

Hybrid vehicles

Public vehicles, such as buses and taxis, would emit a lot less CO_2 if they were hybrids. Constantly stopping and starting, they could run off the electric motor over short distances and then switch to the ordinary engine over longer distances.

Hybrid bus fleets have already taken off in the USA and from 2012 new buses in London will be hybrids. The engineering company Evo Electric says that a taxi with an electric motor would decrease its petrol use by about 60 per cent, and suggests that existing taxis be retrofitted with this technology.

Greener trains

Although most trains in Sweden run on hydro-electricity, a 'green train' is being developed. With the help of a magnet propulsion engine and a system to improve traction, this new train will use 30 per cent less power than a standard model. In China, the end of 2010 will see the arrival of a fleet of 300 diesel-electric trains with 84 per cent less emissions than most trains already in operation.

Questions and activities

1. Do you agree with the congestion charge to make driving 'less attractive'? What other measures could be taken?

2. Note every journey you and your family make by car in a week. Which journeys could have been made in a low-carbon way?

Cheap flights forever?

Flying on the cheap seems great, but air travel is the fastest-growing source of carbon emissions. Airlines are working hard on fuel efficiency, alternative fuels and emissions trading to cut their carbon output, but can they do enough in time?

Jet streams

Roughly 2 per cent of global CO_2 emissions come from aviation – in wealthier nations, such as the UK, it's 7 per cent. With the number of passengers expected to double by 2025, air travel is the fastest-growing source of greenhouse-gas emissions. Sian Foster from Virgin Atlantic gave our research team an insider's look at how the aviation industry plans to address its contribution to global warming.

Using less fuel

A number of airlines are cutting their passengers' carbon footprint with fuel efficiency. 'By 2020,' says Foster, 'Virgin Atlantic has committed to reducing its CO_2 emissions per passenger kilometre by 30 per cent.' The airline plans to reduce its emissions by investing in planes with higher fuel-efficiency, flying them more efficiently and reducing on-board weight.

Along with other airlines and governments, Virgin is also working on the One European Sky project, which would coordinate air space to allow planes to take more direct routes to their destinations. 'An average European airline,' Foster tells us, 'could cut its CO_2 emissions by 10 per cent if air space were better organised.' Fuel and other efficiencies help in cutting emissions, but as long as aircraft are dependent on oil, flying will remain an unsustainable mode of travel. Are alternative low-carbon fuels available?

Hydrogen for aviation

Electric batteries today are far from good enough to power passenger planes, but hydrogen shows promise. Boeing, the aerospace company, successfully flew a small propeller plane using a hydrogen fuel cell in 2008. 'While this is encouraging,' says Foster, 'Virgin aren't pursuing hydrogen, and the feeling is that it won't be a real possibility on passenger planes for 40 years.'

Which biofuel?

According to Foster, 'Biofuels are the alternative fuels of choice for the aviation industry.' Some of the world's largest airlines have successfully tested a mixture of second-generation biofuels and normal jet fuel in their planes. Foster reveals that 5 per cent of Virgin's fuel will come from second-generation biofuels by 2015.

However, Virgin sees these as just stepping-stones. 'What the whole industry is really excited about,' says Foster, 'is algae, which doesn't have the same environmental worries as second-generation biofuels.' Algae, the third generation of biofuel, has had some promising tests and it's being

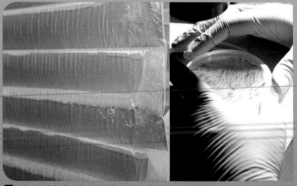

⬆ Algae biofuel - the future of air travel?

backed by big-name investors, like Bill Gates. Air France-KLM is leading the way, with hopes for 7 per cent of its fuel to come from algae by 2010.

Too little, too late?

A jumbo jet run primarily on algae fuel has never been flown. By the time it is fully developed, goes through all the safety tests and producers are able to make enough algae to replace ordinary jet fuel, experts say it could be the year 2040. If oil remains the dominant aviation fuel until then, CO_2 emissions from air travel could still be rising.

Paying for pollution

Foster, however, points out that 'airlines cannot afford to allow their emissions to rise for much longer – literally.' After 2012, the EU Emissions Trading Scheme will cover all flights within, into and out of the European Union. This means that CO_2 produced by airlines over and above a certain carbon allowance will have to be paid for by airlines and therefore ultimately by passengers.

'Virgin Atlantic and other airlines are calling for governments to agree an environmentally ambitious target for the whole aviation industry,' says Foster. This would include aviation emissions in international reduction targets. 'The idea,' she says, 'is that airlines will have to pay such a high price for pollution that they will have to quickly cut their emissions or else face bankruptcy.'

Questions and activities

1. Give three reason why air travel is expected to double by 2025. What are the pros and cons of more air travel?

2. Is it a good idea to make planes pay for their emissions?

Alternatives to air travel

We are constantly made to feel guilty about wanting to fly to distant parts of the world, but what are the alternatives? In fact, already there are several and, in our post-carbon future, there may be many more.

From sky to land

Aeroplanes cruise at around 900 km/h. Although a number of countries are well serviced by high-speed trains travelling at over 250 km/h, they are scarce in most of the world. There are planes from Beijing to Europe that take less than half a day, but to travel the same route on existing trains could take two weeks. Energy expert George Monbiot believes that it would be possible to build an intercontinental network of fast, low-carbon trains as early as 2030. Failing that, travel by slow train would often remain the best available alternative to air travel.

Did you know?

Taking the Eurostar train from Paris to London emits 90 per cent less CO₂ than the same trip by plane.

Flying free

*Going somewhere new
where the sea sparkles blue,
where trees are greener,
beaches cleaner
I love to fly!*

*But far away...
hurricanes, heatwaves,
rising sea, flash floods.*

*For a while, denial.
Not my fault...
Or is it my responsibility?
My jolly jaunts partly to blame?*

*So I quit my holiday habit
that was killing the planet.
It's trains and buses for me,
in a new kind of life,
where I'm flying free.*

Candia Crosfield

To sea

Although more comfortable and sometimes cheaper, crossing oceans in ships travelling at 54 km/h will never be as quick as flying. And given the fuel consumption of an average ocean liner, sea travel won't do much to cut your carbon footprint. But the shipping industry is looking to enter the post-carbon age by building dual-fuel ships, with large fixed sails as well as engines.

⬆ Over nine million people use the Eurostar each year.

Back to the sky

Emitting 90 per cent less CO_2 than jets, airships could be the low-carbon answer for air travel. Airships are large blimps inflated with helium gas, which lifts them to cruise at 1,500 m at speeds of 150 km/h. Michael Stewart, from World SkyCat, told our research team why he believes airships can play a significant role in the post-carbon future...

Airships versus ships and planes

'Though it takes 40 hours to travel from New York to the UK by airship, it will be a fantastic experience!' says Stewart. 'Passengers will be able to move around like on an ocean liner, visit restaurants and a cinema, but it would be three times faster than a ship. With the capacity to carry 200 tonnes of cargo, you could take your car with you!' Stewart thinks airships could compete with shipping for cargo as well as passengers.

Not there yet

Airship technology is tried and tested, but there are almost none in the sky today. At US$200 million each, they're a big investment, but Stewart thinks take-off is around the corner. 'Airships can land and take off almost anywhere – an airport, a field, a lake. My ambition is to have SkyCats shuttling people to the London Olympics in 2012.'

Beneath the ground

In 1972, the US Patent Office issued a patent to the US Atomic Energy Authority for a nuclear tunnelling machine that melts rock and earth, vitrifying it into a glass-lined, perfectly sealed tunnel as it moves forward. Known as a 'Subterrene', it tunnels much faster than a conventional machine, at 10–11 km/h, leaving no debris behind. Subterrenes make it possible to plan a global water grid, carrying water from the water-rich north to the thirsty south. They could also create a high-speed passenger network of flying pods for more than 200 passengers. Impelled by electromagnets at up to 3000 km/h down vacuum-sealed tunnels, the journey from London to Sydney could take three hours. Possible? Maybe – and surely better to travel at zero gravity underground than to use tonnes of fuel to hoist 200 tonnes of aircraft 9,000 m into the sky?

Questions and activities

1. Do you disagree with anything in the poem 'Flying free'? Write your own poem in response.

2. Do you think airships will ever compete with planes, ships and trains? Why/why not?

one planet living

⬆ Ways to give one planet the breathing space it needs.

Zero-carbon housing, renewable energy, public transport ... how does it all fit into the big picture of a post-carbon future? One Planet Living tries to bring together all the elements of our post-carbon future in a single overall vision of sustainability.

Just one planet

If everyone in the world consumed as many natural resources as the average person in Europe, we'd need three planets to support us. If everyone consumed as much as the average North American, we would need five planets. Taken together, the human race is currently consuming resources as if it had 1.3 planets to sustain it. One Planet Living (OPL), the philosophy of conservation organisation WWF and eco-charity BioRegional, gives 10 principles of sustainability to guide communities and individuals everywhere towards living wholesome, modern lives within the limits of one planet.

A one planet life

*America, Asia, Africa, Australia and
Europe too,
we can either save our planet
or
live as we do.*

*We must recycle, reduce and reuse.
We must cut down on fossil fuels.*

*We must learn to take less, so we can give,
give more to others
so they can live.*

Sarah Lacey, Ireland

Principle	One Planet Living
1. Zero carbon	We must strive to emit no CO_2. This means energy-efficient buildings and appliances supplied with zero-carbon energy. OPL communities should supply their own carbon-free energy where possible to speed up the move from fossil fuels.
2. Zero waste	Reduce, reuse, recycle and repair. For OPL, people must practise these four Rs. OPL projects need to provide facilities where people can compost food waste and recycle anything they need to throw away.
3. Sustainable transport	OPL projects should encourage people to use low-carbon forms of transport by providing them with alternatives wherever possible.
4. Local and sustainable materials	To reduce the impact of construction, OPL communities should be built with as many recycled materials as possible. To minimise the distance that these materials need to be transported, they should be sourced locally.
5. Local and sustainable food	Local and organic food produce should be encouraged and made available in OPL communities. This would be better for our land, reduce the need for packaging and almost eliminate the carbon footprint of our food from transport.
6. Sustainable water	Water is a scarce resource and it must be conserved. Using it efficiently, recycling it and collecting rainwater for use in buildings are some of the key conservation strategies.
7. Natural habitats and wildlife	OPL means protecting existing habitats and wildlife from human activities and creating new, safe habitats to conserve endangered species.
8. Culture and heritage	Communities often become global citizens at the expense of their own local identity. Preserving and building on traditions can sustain local identity, which is important for community well-being.
9. Equity and fair trade	By addressing poverty locally and supporting practices such as fair trade between nations, OPL communities can bring about a more just world.
10. Health and happiness	OPL communities should facilitate and promote the physical, mental and spiritual well-being of all its residents.

BedZED – a way forward

Developed by the eco-charity BioRegional, BedZed is a community just outside London dedicated to the principles of One Planet Living. BioRegional co-founder Sue Riddlestone gave our research team a tour of BedZED and answered our questions.

Why the name BedZED?

It stands for Beddington Zero Energy Development. We call it 'zero energy' because BedZED homes are designed to have no CO_2 emissions. Built with highly effective insulation materials, they require little heating, and energy-efficient appliances help ensure that residents use almost half as much electricity as an average UK household. Energy comes from a large array of solar panels and a small on-site power plant, run on waste wood, also provides homes with continuous hot water.

Does BedZED address the environmental impact of housing construction and maintenance?

We were able to make the construction process for BedZED almost one-third less carbon intensive with the help of reclaimed materials, like timber and steel, from older buildings. And to help consumers maintain their homes in a way that satisfies One Planet Living principles, BioRegional has teamed up with hardware store B&Q to put out a range of almost 2,000 sustainable products.

How does BedZED reduce individual emissions from transport?

BedZED encourages people to travel less by being close to schools, shops and jobs. To reduce car ownership, it is connected to public transport and has the UK's first 'car club' – a scheme allowing club members to rent a car at an hourly rate.

What about emissions from consumer goods and food?

We encourage simply buying less 'stuff' as the most sustainable option. Where possible, we arrange the provision of goods and services that minimise the impact of consumption. For example, 86 per cent of our residents regularly buy organic food, provided by local producers.

What are BedZED's stratagies to reduce water consumption and deal with household waste?

Taps and showers in BedZED are water efficient and we also collect and reuse rainwater. Compared to the average UK home, BedZED residents have cut water usage per person from 150 litres per day to 72 litres. Sixty per cent of our resident's waste is either composted or recycled.

CO₂ emissions of the average European resident					
Housing	Home energy	Transport	Food	Consumer goods	Government & business
8%	23%	23%	8%	13%	25%

⬆ The government and business services people use are responsible for a quarter of their carbon footprint. BedZED helps people reduce the other three-quarters of their CO₂ emissions under their control.

Does BedZED contribute to the well-being of residents?

A survey of BedZED households found that people really appreciated the sense of community – average residents know 20 neighbours by name, compared to the regional average of eight. The survey also showed that people were happy with BedZED's facilities, which include sports amenities, a crèche, health-care centre and a café.

To what extent has BedZED achieved One Planet Living?

We're not there yet, but we've learned a lot. One of the greatest lessons BedZED has to teach is that individual behaviour is the real key to One Planet Living. By making the effort to live sustainably, some residents have more than halved their CO_2 emissions, for example. Other residents, however, travel a lot by plane or car and fail to use the recycling facilities.

So we can expect to see more eco-communities?

Many more we hope – and around the world, too. Currently, BioRegional is helping to develop eco-communities in the UK, the USA, Portugal, South Africa and the world's first eco-city, Masdar, in the United Arab Emirates. There's lots going on out there and we're just one part of it.

Questions and activities

1. Would you like to live in a post-carbon community? Why?

2. How would you make BedZED a better post-carbon community?

3. How do you think you could apply One Planet Living to your own life?

Efficient buildings by 2050

Our homes and other buildings are energy guzzlers. They require heating and electricity for inefficient machines and gadgets, giving them unacceptably high CO_2 emissions. Energy efficiency brings their power consumption down to One Planet Living standards.

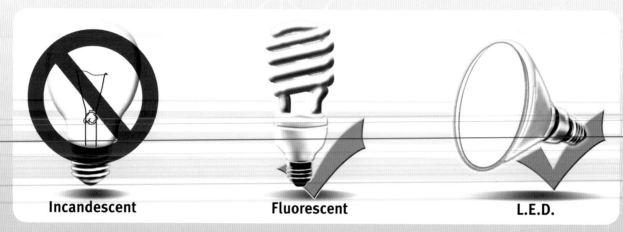

Incandescent   Fluorescent   L.E.D.

Energy guzzlers

Buildings consume 40 per cent of all the energy produced in the world, and are generally supplied with electricity and heat from coal- and gas-fired power stations. This makes them more responsible for CO_2 emissions than anything else. To meet climate-change targets, old and new buildings must halve their energy demand before 2050. This will be difficult to achieve, but we can do it with energy efficiency, which just means cutting down on unnecessary energy waste.

Did you know?

Using energy-efficient bulbs across Europe would save more energy than 10 million people consume in a year.

The road to energy efficiency	
Insulate	The majority of buildings – especially homes – are poorly insulated, meaning that they lose a lot of heat through their walls, windows and roofs. Upgrading them with proper insulation would cut around 40 per cent from a building's energy use.
Use efficient electrical goods	Efficient electrical goods use 20–40 per cent less power than standard models. But it takes a lot of energy to make these goods, too. To maximise the energy and CO_2 savings, an energy-efficient product should be replacing one about 10 years old.
Replace light bulbs	Standard (incandescent) light bulbs are hot to touch because they lose 98 per cent of the energy they consume as heat. In Australia, the USA, Canada and Europe these bulbs are being replaced by fluorescent bulbs and light-emitting diode (LED) lamps, which last 10 times longer and are 75 per cent more efficient.

Pearl River

To meet the 2050 target for buildings, all new structures must be built to have the lowest possible carbon footprint. One of many new buildings blazing the way forward is the 71- storey Pearl River Tower in Guangzhou, China. Once completed, it will be the world's most energy-efficient building. Not only will it use half as much energy as a standard building of the same size, it will also produce all its own renewable energy with inbuilt solar panels, solar water heaters and wind turbines. Key to getting enough power from wind turbines is the curved structure of the building, which helps increase wind speeds by up to two and a half times.

Empire efficient

To halve energy use from buildings by 2050, all our old energy-wasting structures must be upgraded to high energy-efficient standards. New York's Empire State Building, one of the world's tallest structures at 102 storeys, is setting an example by investing US$20 million to reduce its energy consumption by 40 per cent before 2013. This translates to saving 105,000 tonnes of CO_2 a year. The main strategies are adding an extra layer of insulation to its 6,500 windows, placing insulation behind radiators, and upgrading the air-conditioning system with more efficient machines. Through their computers, workers will be able to monitor the energy being consumed by their offices, encouraging them to take responsibility for keeping it to a minimum. Supervisors claim that the cost of the upgrade will be paid back with energy bill savings within three years.

School of tomorrow

Even schools need to get in on the act. Howe Dell primary school, in the east of England, could be the school of the future. It is the first building in the world to use a revolutionary Inter-seasonal Heat Transfer system that stores underground heat from the playground during summertime, releasing it in winter to warm the building. Meanwhile, solar water heaters help provide hot water, and solar panels and a wind turbine generate electricity. Large, strategically placed windows maximise sunlight, reducing the need for lighting. Emissions reductions haven't been measured yet, but they are expected to be great.

Questions and activities

1. Do a survey and find out what kind of bulbs your family, friends and school are using. How many are low-energy and how many are incandescent?

2. You are at a design meeting. Explain the ways you are going to make your new building the most eco-friendly in the world.

Post-carbon cities

Can everyone enjoy a One Planet lifestyle? With half the global population now living in cities, we have to learn how. The new Gulf city of Masdar shows the way: it's the world's first post-carbon city built from scratch. Other cities will need major rebuilding to get close to Masdar's standard of zero-carbon sustainability.

Green city in the desert

The world's most sustainable city is called Masdar, and it's being built in Abu Dhabi, capital of the United Arab Emirates. As the first zero-carbon, zero waste city powered entirely by renewable energy, the city will set the standard for future urban developments. Dr Sultan Al Jaber, leading the Masdar project, hails it as 'the blueprint for the cities of the future'. The buildings will be among the most energy efficient in the world, several actually producing more energy then they consume. The concrete and steel used to build the city comes from recycled materials. Electricity for the 40,000 residents will be generated mostly from solar panels spread across the city's roofs.

Getting around Masdar

With its narrow and well-shaded streets derived from traditional Arabic cities, Masdar city will favour a pedestrian lifestyle. For longer distances, people will travel using the 3,000 automatic and battery-powered four-seater Personal Rapid Transport pods. A light overhead train will connect Masdar with central Abu Dhabi.

Water and waste

Masdar aims to generate zero waste by reusing and recycling all the waste collected. The city will limit water consumption to 8,000 cu m per day through water conservation and reuse. All waste water will be recycled into toilets and for irrigation purposes.

Quality of life

Promoting healthy lifestyles with no street pollution or traffic, the city will offer a high quality of life combined with a low carbon footprint. The Masdar Institute of Science and Technology, located in the heart of the city, will attract researchers, educators, experts and cleantech companies from around the world, creating an environment ripe for innovation.

⬆ Green city in the desert: an artist's vision of Masdar with transport pods and overhead train.

Greening today's cities

For most city-dwellers, living in a post-carbon future won't be as easy as moving into a ready-made, sustainable metropolis like Masdar. Instead, cities must change the way they run. London has committed itself to the ideal of One Planet Living. How could it transform itself to achieve this goal?

Low-carbon travel

Although not quite like future Masdar citizens, Londoners travel beneath their city, too – using an underground system that connects with buses and long-distance trains. Despite having such a good transport network, London is currently congested with an endless stream of polluting road traffic running through it. Promoting car clubs to reduce car ownership and investing in an infrastructure for electric (or even hydrogen) vehicles, would encourage a much greater uptake in low-carbon transport.

Giving bicycles greater priority on the roads and introducing a 'bicing' scheme, like the one in Barcelona, would only further reduce CO_2 emissions. Unless aviation began to drastically reduce its emissions, London would have to limit flights coming in and going out, encouraging low-carbon options like trains or airships instead.

Power houses

From 2016, the law will require all new homes in the UK to be built to zero-carbon standards. This should help bring about a boom in eco-communities on the outskirts of post-carbon London. Existing homes and buildings would be renovated to be energy efficient, while heat pumps and smart meters would further improve efficiency. Power would likely come from offshore wind, coal-fired power plants with carbon capture and storage, some geothermal, and solar power from the Sahara via the super-grid. Systems to collect rainwater should feature in communities and large buildings, while every kind of waste needs to have its own accessible recycling points.

Questions and activities

1. You are an architect asked to design your own version of Masdar. Sketch out a street plan, highlighting the main features.

2. What strategies would you use to make the London Olympics 'the greenest Games yet'?

Changing habits

By becoming environmentally conscious consumers, we can all move towards One Planet Living and make huge reductions in our CO₂ emissions wherever we live. Here are some ideas on how you can help with the transition to the post-carbon future.

Clothes-swap

In the UK, a poll found that there were an estimated 2.4 billion pieces of clothing in British wardrobes that went unworn for 12 months. Meanwhile, the UK discards two million tonnes of clothing each year to make way for the latest fashion. To help reduce the impacts of fashion consumption, why not host or participate in a clothes-swapping party? It gives you an opportunity to meet friends and trade the clothes you don't use for those that you will.

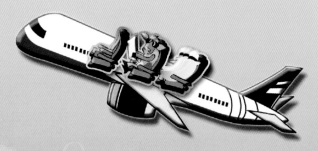

Carbon-friendly food

Wealthy people's demand for out-of-season food throughout the year results in planes, ships and trucks carting goods from one side of the planet to the other seven days a week. This is terrible for the climate. Campaigners in California have adapted the terms 'carnivore' and 'watershed' to encourage people to become 'locavores' and eat within their 'foodshed'. As a rule of thumb, eating locally grown food, in season (not grown in heated greenhouses) is the most carbon-friendly food. Campaigners are now trying to get all food products labelled with their carbon footprint to help consumers make this choice.

Meet Joao

Europeans consume 100 kg of meat each year, one-fifth of which is beef. Cows belch out the greenhouse gas methane and as global demand for beef grows, forests are being destroyed to make way for raising cattle – especially in Brazil. And the 8 kg of grain it takes to produce 1 kg of beef could be used to feed people. For these reasons, I'm a vegetarian and believe that eating less meat must be part of our future.

Joao Scarpelini, Brazil

The carbon cost of meat

The 2006 UK Climate Change Programme reported that, if every person in the UK ate no meat for *one* day a week, the carbon emissions saved would be like taking five million cars off the road or replacing a billion light bulbs with low-energy ones. If they ate no meat for *five* days, it would save an amount equal to the carbon emissions from all household electricity. If they all went vegetarian *seven* days a week, like Joao, they would halve the total UK domestic carbon emissions. So – try being a vegetarian!

Pre-cycling

Better than recycling is avoiding waste in the first place. Try pre-cycling, which consumes a lot less energy than the manufacturing process

Your potential CO₂ savings

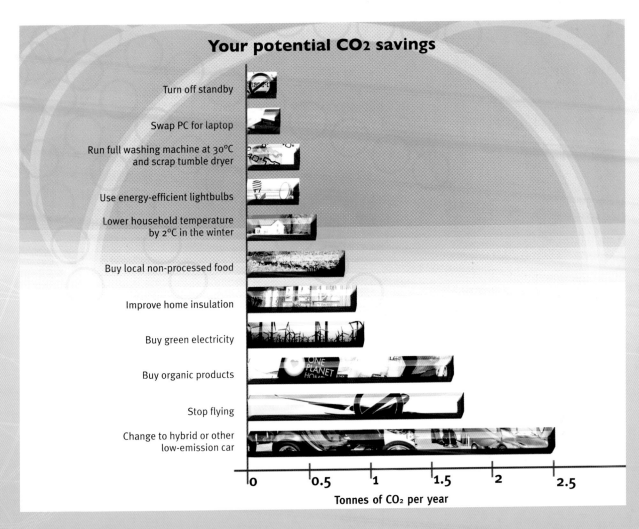

Turn off standby	
Swap PC for laptop	
Run full washing machine at 30°C and scrap tumble dryer	
Use energy-efficient lightbulbs	
Lower household temperature by 2°C in the winter	
Buy local non-processed food	
Improve home insulation	
Buy green electricity	
Buy organic products	
Stop flying	
Change to hybrid or other low-emission car	

Tonnes of CO₂ per year

0   0.5   1   1.5   2   2.5

of recycling. Pre-cycling involves choosing the product with the least packaging (therefore diverting waste from landfill and the recycling bin) and bringing along your own bag. Instead of buying packaged sandwiches, for instance, you could take a lunchbox to school, along with a reusable water bottle.

E-reading

If your home is supplied with power from coal-fired power plants, then reading the newspaper on the computer for 30 minutes makes you responsible for 25 per cent more CO₂ emissions than if you bought a hard copy. Using an e-reader, a hand-held flat-screen device that allows you to get the daily news or read your favourite novel digitally, could halve your carbon footprint from reading newspapers or books.

Questions and activities

1. What else can you do to reduce your carbon footprint and live a more sustainable life?

2. What do you think of Joao's reasons for being a vegetarian? Do you agree that eating less meat should be a part of the future?

Super-green possibilities

Imagine a world of boundless zero-carbon energy, where there is no such thing as waste, and urban centres reconnect with food and nature. Sound like a post-carbon pipe dream? Well, work is underway to make these a reality in the twenty-first century.

Nuclear fusion

Nuclear fusion is the chemical reaction that makes our sun so powerful. Scientists have been able to recreate this reaction on Earth for a moment by generating heat of 100 million°C in a magnetic doughnut-shaped chamber. Fusion could be the answer to all our energy needs forever, if only we could sustain the reaction and design power plants around it.

Scientists from across the globe formed the International Thermonuclear Experimental Reactor (ITER) in 2006 – an intergovernmental project hoping to bring fusion energy to the world in a matter of decades. A nuclear fusion power station would emit no CO_2, produce hardly any radioactive waste, and because the fusion reaction is so difficult to sustain, it couldn't run out of control and cause harm.

Did you know?

France will host the ITER fusion reactor. It will begin testing in 2018 and the project will cost US$16 billion.

Solar space

What about getting our post-carbon power from outer space? Satellite solar panels up to 2 km long have the potential to provide us with all our power demands. In orbit around the globe, these solar panels would have 24-hour access to direct sunlight. Lasers would beam the collected solar energy down to antennas on Earth, which would convert it to electricity. Japan's aerospace programme already has 180 scientists working towards a fully functional satellite solar power station by 2030.

One difficulty with building satellite solar stations is getting the construction materials into space in the first place. For this purpose, experts have suggested building a space elevator, which would eliminate the need for regular rocket launches. Still just an idea, but undergoing serious

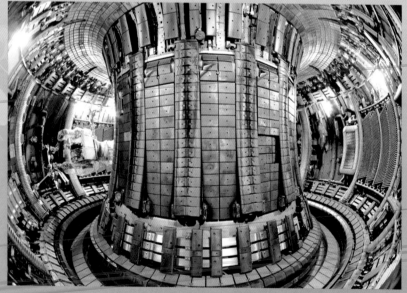

⬆ Inside one of the world's few fusion reactors, at the JET facility in the UK.

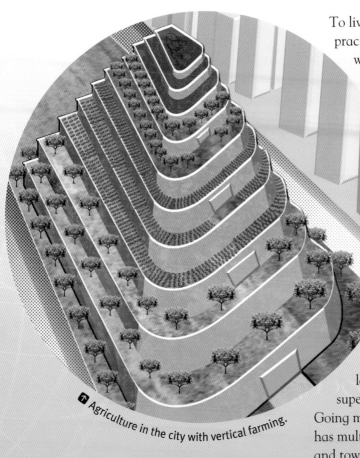
↗ Agriculture in the city with vertical farming.

To live on a truly sustainable planet, these practices would need to become the norm worldwide. And the movement has already begun: communities in the Netherlands and China, and some big-name manufacturers such as Nike, have been amongst the first to adopt cradle to cradle ideals.

Vertical farming

By farming in cities and towns, we could grow more food for a hungry world, and urban dwellers would have greater access to local, organic produce. But where could we find the space for this? One idea, taking off particularly well in New York City, is rooftop farming. This means using the roofs of large building such as apartment blocks, superstores and warehouses to grow crops. Going much further, the 'vertical farming' concept has multi-storey greenhouses being built in cities and towns to provide food for their inhabitants. Although it would cost hundreds of millions to build, Professor Dickson Despommier, who is developing the idea of vertical farms, believes that a 30-storey would feed 50,000 people.

investigation, the elevator would consist of a 1 m wide cable along which robots would climb to space with their deliveries.

Cradle to cradle

William McDonough and Michael Braungart have become famous for their concept of 'cradle to cradle', which is a model of society where everything gets recycled. The big idea is that manufacturers should design all products – from carpets to furniture to stereos – in such a way that they can be returned and easily made into other products for resale. On this model, a computer would never make its way to the landfill: its parts would have continual rebirths as newer computer parts. The same goes for organic waste, which would be collected and recycled as fertiliser.

Questions and activities

1. How do you react to the ideas of building fusion reactors and solar panels in space by means of a space elevator?

2. Why do you think societies haven't yet adopted the cradle to cradle model of recycling?

3. Are vertical farms a realistic idea? What advantages and disadvantages can you see?

Geo-engineering – a last resort?

Geo-engineering means interfering with the Earth's climate system on a planetary scale. Unless we quickly build the post-carbon future and send our CO_2 emissions into steep decline, experts believe that we won't be able to stop dangerous global warming without it. What would that look like?

Reflecting the sun

Most of the effects of global warming could be prevented if only less sunlight were to reach the Earth's surface. One way this could be achieved is for ships to spray seawater into the sky. Tiny salt crystals would form, increasing the clouds' reflective power against the sun. For this geo-engineering strategy, 1,500 ships with spraying equipment would need to launch 1.4 billion tonnes of seawater towards the skies each year.

Sulphur dioxide (SO_2) in the atmosphere slightly scatters sunlight and has an overall cooling effect on the planet. Although this gas can damage the ozone layer, a popular idea is to spread millions of tonnes of SO_2 across the atmosphere each year, using aeroplanes.

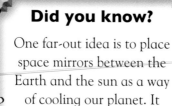

Did you know?

One far-out idea is to place space mirrors between the Earth and the sun as a way of cooling our planet. It would cost around US$5 trillion to complete.

Biochar

Plants, trees and other organic materials emit CO_2 as they decompose. Cooking them in airless ovens makes charcoal, or biochar, which locks in the carbon. Enthusiasts suggest that plantations of fast-growing trees could be used to capture carbon, which could then be cut down, turned to biochar, buried and replanted again – continually taking carbon from the atmosphere and storing it in the ground. Exploratory projects are ongoing in places like Cameroon and Mongolia to determine the environmental impacts of biochar plantations.

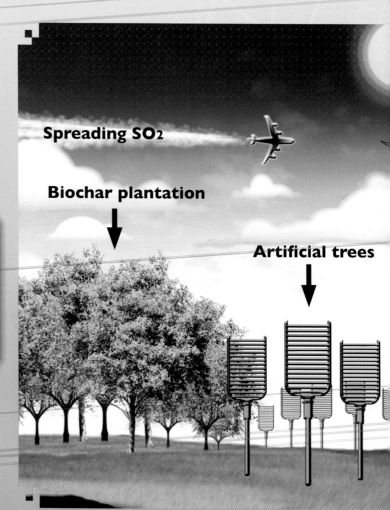

Spreading SO_2

Biochar plantation

Artificial trees

Artificial trees

Looking like giant fly swatters, artificial trees would have 'leaves' designed to extract CO_2 from the air using carbon-capturing chemicals. Captured carbon would be piped to an underground storage site. Professor Klaus Lackner, who is developing the trees, believes that each one could absorb the annual CO_2 emissions of 20,000 cars.

Ocean fertilisation

Spreading iron filings across the ocean provides fertiliser for phytoplankton, which absorb and store CO_2. The effects of interfering with ocean chemistry in this way are unknown and potentially dangerous – it could increase the acidity of our already too acidic waters. However, experiments in the Southern Ocean have tested out ocean fertilisation, capturing carbon with limited success.

Risky business

Geo-engineering makes even geo-engineers uneasy: Professor Daniel Schrag recognises that we don't understand our environment well enough to manipulate it on a large scale, but he thinks the risks are worth it, given the global-warming alternative. The extent to which geo-engineering will need to play a role in preventing climate change depends on how quickly we put an end to our carbon emissions.

Earth engineering

O to be a tree-maker,
a super-science-hero,
shadowing the Earth,
playing with clouds.

Nature creates us.
Do we dare control nature?
If I was World President…
and the Arctic was collapsing…
would I accept the dare?

Eugenia Capalbo, Argentina

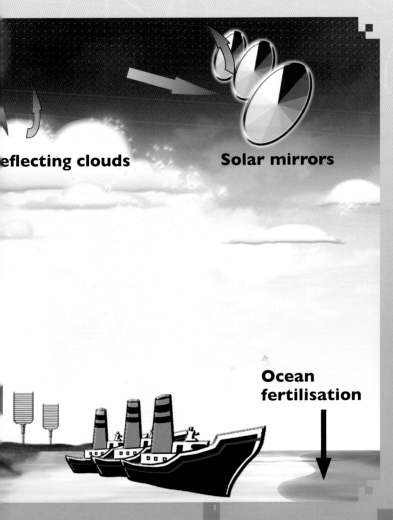

eflecting clouds

Solar mirrors

Ocean fertilisation

Questions and activities

1. Should we begin with geo-engineering projects now or should it be our very last resort in tackling global warming?

2. You are an investor, convinced that geo-engineering must play a role in tackling climate change: Which geo-engineering strategies would you invest in?

section 3

action: making it happen

post-carbon actors

We've seen the post-carbon solutions. Now, we need to figure out who is going make it all happen. Think about a pyramid of four groups of actors, with lawmakers at the top, big business and local government in the middle, and individual citizens – that's you and me – at the bottom. In the pages that follow, we will look at how each group of actors is planning and working to build our post-carbon future.

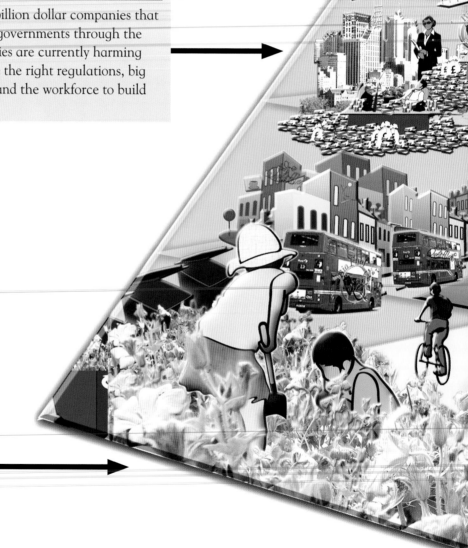

Big business

These are the banks and the multi-billion dollar companies that run our industries and help finance governments through the taxes they pay. Some of their activities are currently harming the planet, but if governments make the right regulations, big business has the finances, the skills and the workforce to build the post-carbon future.

YOU and ME

Individuals hold up the whole pyramid! We may just be the extras in this epic story but, in the crowd scenes, we are the ones making the most noise. With our votes and voices, we have the power to make or break governments, while our consumer habits and lifestyle choices can either support or bankrupt big businesses. Also, individuals around the globe are coming up with all sorts of innovations to help make the transition to a post-carbon future.

The lawmakers

Top of the bill, in the superstar role, we have national governments and intergovernmental organisations such as the United Nations (UN) and the European Union (EU). Informed by up-to-date scientific reports on climate change, the UN tries to get governments to agree on laws and regulations to deal with the threat of climate change.

Local actors

Local governments, local organisations and small businesses are the bit-part actors – working locally to implement the policies determined at higher levels. Local laws, local taxes, local and regional one-planet living initiatives and local farms and manufacturers are the critical building blocks of a sustainable, post-carbon future.

lawmakers and big business

The traffic light turns red, you stop. It turns green, you go. That's the law. We drive on the correct side of the road. We pay our taxes. That's the law – and if we disobey the law, cars crash, people are killed. Society falls apart. It's the same for climate change. If we are to stop catastrophic climate change, we must start with laws – global, regional, national and local laws.

Kyoto Protocol

Since the Earth Summit in Brazil in 1992, the world's governments have recognised that they must unite to combat climate change. The United Nations has led the process. The Kyoto Protocol, agreed in 1997 by 183 countries, is the most important treaty agreed so far. Amongst many features – carbon offsetting, adaptation funds, and others – the main one required industrialised countries to reduce their emissions by 5 per cent from what they were in 1990. The US government, however, rejected the Kyoto Protocol and many countries are failing to meet their 5 per cent target.

Beyond Kyoto: Copenhagen

The Kyoto Protocol expires in 2012 and has to be replaced. Negotiations for a new protocol are to be finalised in Denmark's capital, Copenhagen, in December 2009. Governments are expected to agree to an 80 per cent cut in global CO_2 emissions by 2050. Several experts believe that far more drastic cuts are needed to keep global warming below 2°C. But making climate change laws is fiendishly complicated – especially when they have to be agreed by 193 governments. And, once agreed, it is almost harder to get governments, and their citizens, to obey them.

What the world needs

What the world needs is –
To take action on climate change
To set targets and pass laws
To invest in renewables
To reduce energy consumption
To make us pay for pollution!

What the world needs is –
To wake up!
We only have one planet
And we cannot replace it,
Once it is gone.

Cast of *Kids on Strike*, Rochester, USA

Putting a price on carbon

One effective way of reducing emissions is to put a price, or a tax, on carbon. When governments wanted to get motorists to use unleaded fuels, the transition was made simple by raising the tax on leaded fuels, making unleaded fuels cheaper. Another way is to sell permits to emit carbon at safe levels. These permits can be bought and sold by companies or nations, benefiting those with lower emissions, and creating a potentially massive carbon trading market. A third way is called 'carbon offsetting'. The Kyoto Protocol included several ways for countries to offset their carbon emissions. One is called the Clean Development Mechanism (CDM) which would, for example, allow a German construction company to offset (reduce) its carbon emissions by building a wind farm in a developing country. Copenhagen will expand all these ways of making polluters pay.

REDD

Reducing Emissions from Deforestation and Forest Degradation (REDD) is a UN scheme designed to ensure that communities can profit from conserving forests, rather than cutting them down. Funded by aid, carbon markets etc., REDD will be included in the Copenhagen protocol.

Adaptation Fund

Wealthy countries have to help developing nations adapt to climate change. Kyoto set up an Adaptation Fund to help them build flood defences etc. To date, support for the fund has been feeble. Developing countries hope that Copenhagen will raise it to around US$100 billion a year.

Environmental Security Council

Currently, the world has no way to enforce environmental laws. With climate change now killing more people than conventional wars, some have suggested that the UN Security Council should become an Environmental Security Council. Sadly, most governments have little appetite for surrendering their power to such a council. That could change in our lifetimes: do you think there ought to be a way that the UN global family can punish any of its members that wilfully allows its people or industries to pollute and kill?

⬆ An activist at UN climate talks gets his message across.

Questions and activities

1. Why do you think governments might be reluctant to sign up to UN climate treaties? What pressures do they face?

2. Is carbon offsetting a good idea?

National governments

In the absence of an Environmental Security Council or binding UN law, national governments must police climate change and regulate the energy revolution. Some nations are ahead of the game, pledging carbon neutrality, while the big polluters are cleaning up their act.

Carbon neutrality

Carbon neutrality means achieving net zero CO_2 emissions. Some countries propose to achieve this by slashing their emissions and offsetting those they cannot cut by voluntarily buying carbon credits or contributing to carbon-cutting projects through the UN's Clean Development Mechanism. Three developed countries have committed to going carbon neutral so far – Norway (by 2030), New Zealand (by 2040) and Iceland (by 2050). Two developing nations, the Maldives and Costa Rica, are likely to be the first.

⬆ Angaga island in the Maldives. Will our CO_2 emissions sink it?

Meet Hamza

My home country, the Maldives, is a group of coral islands in the Indian Ocean in danger of sinking under rising sea levels. Our president, Mohamed Nasheed, announced in 2009 that we would become the world's first carbon neutral nation by 2019. I echo his message to the world: 'Please don't be stupid... If the world can't save countries like the Maldives today, we won't be able to save places like London or New York tomorrow.'

Hamza Khaleel, Maldives

Costa Rica

Just behind the Maldives comes Costa Rica, with a commitment to be carbon neutral by 2021. Forest cover in Costa Rica was 80 per cent in 1950 but by 1987 it was down to just 21 per cent. One of its main carbon-neutrality strategies has been to drastically cut its emissions, while engaging in an aggressive reforestation programme. Today, forest cover in Costa Rica is back up to over 50 per cent.

Big emitters are on board

The three biggest greenhouse-gas emitters – China, the USA and the EU – have not set carbon-neutral goals, but they are showing commitment to tackling climate change. Meanwhile, the UK's Low-Carbon Transition Plan has been hailed as the 'most systematic response to climate change of any major developed economy.' Let's take a look at what these economies are doing to move towards a post-carbon future.

China

China is setting itself up to become a green superpower. Already it makes most of the world's solar panels and wind turbines, its car manufacturers are pushing ahead with electric vehicles, and carbon capture and storage is being developed. By 2020, China should have a super-grid with at least 18 per cent of its energy coming from renewables – more than a tenfold increase from 2009. Government investments totalling US$440 billion will help make all this possible.

USA

Although the USA did not ratify the Kyoto Protocol, President Obama is a key figure negotiating the agreement that will replace it. Already, Obama has announced the USA's intention to spend US$150 billion over 10 years to help build a post-carbon future, creating around 2.5 million green jobs. California is one of the leading US states combating climate change, aiming to cut 25 per cent of its current emissions by 2020.

European Union

The EU has committed itself to cutting its greenhouse-gas emissions by 20 per cent by 2020. Under a new UN protocol, this target could rise to 30 per cent. There are now over 3.4 million jobs in the EU's post-carbon economy, more than in polluting industries. Green investment is booming, while Germany and Spain are the green stars of Europe as world leaders in solar and wind energy.

UK low-carbon transition plan

The UK's Department for Energy and Climate Change has a plan to cut CO_2 emissions by 34 per cent by 2020. Smart-grids, infrastructure for charging electric cars, 15 new eco-towns and the creation of 1.2 million green jobs are all part of it. By 2020, 40 per cent of UK electricity will be from low-carbon sources, and the average new car will emit 40 per cent less CO_2.

Questions and activities

1. What would be the key strategies to make your country the first to go carbon neutral?

2. What are your reactions to Hamza's quote from the president of the Maldives?

3. Why do you think China is becoming a bigger polluter, while at the same time becoming a world leader in renewables?

Greening business

Big business has driven all major industrial revolutions – cars, aviation, computers. The energy revolution is no exception. Look at the chart: investment in clean energy has more than tripled in four years! And 86 per cent of that investment has come from big business, so inevitably it has a huge role in building our post-carbon future.

Turning tides

Peter Lacy, from business analysts Accenture, told our research team that 'the tides are turning in the board rooms of big business as they begin to recognise the need either to be part of the post-carbon future, or else get left behind.' Nowhere is this clearer than in the car industry. Toyota, which invested heavily in hybrid and electric vehicles at the turn of the century, is now the world's biggest car-maker. General Motors, which didn't, was the biggest all through the twentieth century. In 2009, it went bankrupt. Ford's 'recovery plan', designed to pull the company out of its financial crisis, aims to have up to 25 per cent of its cars electric by 2020.

The carbon trading business

As governments put a price on carbon, introducing carbon taxes and making polluters pay for their emissions, a massive new market is emerging to buy and sell carbon-emission permits. In Europe, this is called the Emissions Trading System (ETS). ETS did have start-up problems, but it's now beginning to function effectively. In the USA, there are plans for a 'cap and trade' system – capping emissions at an agreed level and trading the rest. With the financial crisis, many stock-brokers smell big business opportunities in the carbon-trading markets. In 2005, the World Bank valued the carbon market at US$10 billion, with carbon valued at US$10–15 a tonne. If, as analysts believe, the price of carbon rises to US$75–100 a tonne, carbon trading will be a US$100 billion business, creating thousands of jobs!

⊡ Clean energy investments grew from US$35 billion to US$155 billion in just four years. Growth slowed considerably in 2008 because of a global economic downturn. With the help of government stimulus packages, rapid growth is expected once again beyond 2010.

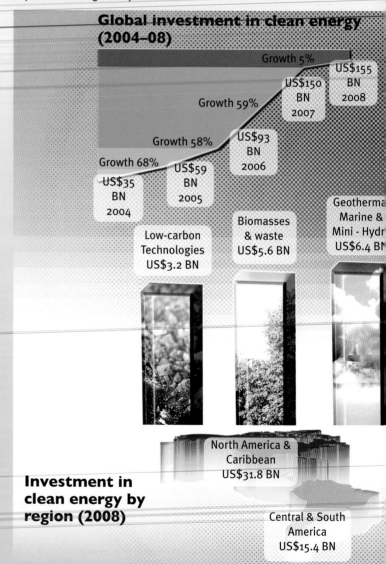

Global investment in clean energy (2004–08)

Growth 5%

US$155 BN 2008

US$150 BN 2007

Growth 59%

US$93 BN 2006

Growth 58%

US$59 BN 2005

Growth 68%

US$35 BN 2004

Low-carbon Technologies US$3.2 BN

Biomasses & waste US$5.6 BN

Geotherma Marine & Mini - Hydr US$6.4 BN

North America & Caribbean US$31.8 BN

Investment in clean energy by region (2008)

Central & South America US$15.4 BN

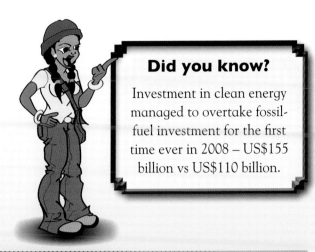

Did you know?

Investment in clean energy managed to overtake fossil-fuel investment for the first time ever in 2008 – US$155 billion vs US$110 billion.

Who's afraid of a post-carbon future?

Some of the biggest companies in the coal, oil and gas industries have been accused of placing obstacles in the way of a post-carbon future, keeping the world dependent on their fuel supply. In the first quarter of 2009, for instance, the USA's fossil-fuel industries spent US$76.1 million on advertising campaigns in an intense effort to kill President Obama's Climate Bill, out-spending environmental groups by 10 to one. Evan Tracey, founder of Campaign Media Analysis, said: 'There's an awful lot of people with an awful lot of money to lose in a post-carbon future, and they have been acting accordingly.' Equally, there's an awful lot of money to be made in post-carbon technologies, and visionary businesses are investing in them.

Vestas

Vestas is one such business. It has been building wind turbines since 1979. Now, with 20,000 employees, an annual turnover of US$6 billion and 28 per cent of the market for wind, it is the world's largest manufacturer of wind turbines. Vestas has already installed over 33,000 turbines in 63 countries. Wind power is a proven technology: wind turbines pay for themselves in two years. Already investments in wind are almost double those in solar, and analysts believe they will grow tenfold by 2020. A good business to be in.

Investment in clean energy by sector (2008)

Biofuels US$20.7 BN

Solar US$31.1 BN

Wind US$52.9 BN

Europe US$49.1 BN

Asia US$20.5 BN

Middle East & Africa US$2.6 BN

Oceania US$0.5 BN

Questions and activities

1. You are president of an oil company. What would make you invest in post-carbon products instead of oil?

2. Why is it significant that renewable investment beat fossil-fuel investment in 2008?

Acting Up

COMMUNITY ACTION

Communities, whether big cities or small villages, can take the lead away from national governments and big business through their own initiatives. Working together at grassroots level, we can turn our communities into post-carbon models of sustainability. Here's a small sample of what's being done.

TRANSITION TOWNS

Starting in 2005 with the town of Kinsale in rural Ireland and moving on to Totnes in the UK, permaculture teacher Rob Hopkins founded the 'transition towns' movement. Hopkins believes that concerned citizens must take the lead in every community to begin the transition to a post-carbon future. By first educating themselves on the issues and then connecting with local governments, businesses, organisations and the community at large, he wants to see each community develop and implement its own post-carbon strategy.

In a short time, the movement has gone global, boasting around 200 officially recognised transition towns in 14 countries – with New Zealand, Italy, the USA and the UK particularly keen to get involved. All sorts of initiatives are underway: sustainability programmes to educate people on how to live a post-carbon life; introducing local currencies to encourage individuals to buy locally produced goods; setting up community gardens; upgrading inefficient buildings, and much more.

[Get with the transition, visit www.transitiontowns.org]

KITENGELA GLASS COMMUNITY

Kitengela Glass is a group of art studios in Kenya with the philosophy 'Recycle everything, pay fair wages, protect our environment.' Its artists collect glass, scrap iron and other waste materials and craft them into all sorts of jewellery, homeware and other artwork for sale. Most of the studio's electricity is provided by solar panels and it uses second-hand packaging. By applying the talent of artists to waste, Kitengela Glass has created a successful business that uses its profits to support an orphanage and plant trees.

SOLAR CITY

Ever since the 1970s, when the city of Freiburg in south-west Germany successfully protested against an attempt to build a nuclear power plant nearby, it has had to find other ways of meeting its increasing electricity needs. Making homes up to 75 per cent more energy efficient and pursuing renewable energy have been key strategies. Few places have adopted solar panels and solar water heaters to the same extent as Freiburg. To the fascination of tourists, inhabitants can be seen decorating thousands of homes and other buildings, from churches to soccer stadiums. Noted for its 500 km of bicycle lanes, low rate of car usage, open spaces and its commitment to renewable energy, Freiburg is recognised as one of the greenest communities in the world.

RECYCLING FOR JAPAN

How many types of waste do you recycle? Three, four, five...? Residents in the village of Kamikatsu in south-western Japan are setting an example for the rest of the world, sorting their waste into 34 different categories as part of their weekly routine. This scheme was adopted to eliminate the need for incinerators and landfills, and ultimately to have a 100 per cent recycling rate (zero waste) by 2020.

LET'S DO IT

Illegal dumping by both industry and ordinary individuals has been degrading woodlands in the eastern European country of Estonia for decades. In 2008, a group of concerned citizens did what the government could not. Setting up a campaign called 'Let's Do It', they decided to clean up the decades of waste – in just one day. By identifying dumping sites of all sizes and engaging with the national media, they were able to mobilise 40,000 volunteers to move 10,000 tonnes of waste, and clean up the whole country in just a few hours.

← Community works to clean up Estonia.

GLOBAL COMMUNITY

Playing a part in our local community, we must not forget that we are also members of a wider, global community. Different organisations have played an important role in encouraging people from around the world to unite as a global community and speak up for the future of our planet. Here are just a few exciting global initiatives.

WORLD ENVIRONMENT DAY

Organised by the United Nations Environment Programme (UNEP), World Environment Day has been taking place on 5 June every year since 1974. Each year explores a different issue – with past themes including desertification, saving the seas and the post-carbon future. Politicians, celebrities, environmental organisations and millions of people in communities across the world highlight each year's theme with cycling parades, art competitions, film festivals, speeches, concerts – anything that raises awareness about the issue in their country.

[It's never too early prepare for World Environment Day, visit www.unep.org]

EARTH HOUR

WWF, the global conservation organisation, has been active in protecting the environment for decades. It is now well known for bringing the world together with Earth Hour. This event takes place on the last Saturday of March between 8.30 and 9.30 p.m. (local time) each year. Households, government buildings, businesses and monuments including the Eiffel Tower and Sydney's Opera House, are encouraged to turn off all non-essential lighting for one hour to raise awareness of climate change. Over 4,000 cities and an estimated one billion people took part in Earth Hour 2009 – the largest climate-change action ever!

[Locate WWF in your region and find out more: www.wwf.org]

BILLIONS OF TREES

Established in 2007 by Kenyan conservationist Wangari Maathai and UNEP, the Billion Tree Campaign promotes reducing the level of CO_2 in the atmosphere, and making the world a greener place, by planting at least a billion trees each year. Communities, businesses and governments around the world are encouraged to do their bit – reporting their activities to UNEP. By June 2009, over four billion trees had been planted across 166 countries – Ethiopia contributing the largest number with 687 million trees planted in 2008 alone, closely followed by Turkey.

[www.unep.org/billiontreecampaign]

⬆ Students in Nagpur, India, show their support for 350 parts per million.

350.ORG

350.org is an organisation with one message: governments must agree on a stronger climate deal than that with which they are proposing to replace the Kyoto Protocol. An agreement that will reduce CO_2 levels in the atmosphere to a safe 350 parts per million, as opposed to a more risky 450 parts per million. 350.org is now famous for its creative way of raising awareness. Churches have rung their bells 350 times, children have planted 350 trees, 350 scuba divers went diving at the Great Barrier Reef, Buddhists in the Himalayas spelt out 350 with their bodies. Thousands of events like these took place across more than 100 countries in 2008 and 2009. They were photographed and uploaded to the 350.org website, resulting in a powerful photographic petition from the people of the world to our leaders, demanding that they agree to strive for safe levels of CO_2 in the atmosphere.

[Visit www.350.org to get involved in future events]

P@SSPORT

Run by WWF, 'P@ssport' is a worldwide virtual network of individuals who bring their voices together in standing up for the planet. Once an issue is highlighted in the WWF network, P@ssport holders begin to take action. In 2008, for instance, a petition signed by 13,000 international P@ssport members pressured the authorities in Hong Kong to save part of its collapsing marine ecosystem by banning commercial fishing. Building up an international community of environmentally conscious individuals can act as a powerful tool for protecting our planet and raising global awareness of the problems it faces.

[To become a P@ssport holder, visit www.panda.org]

PRACTICAL YOUTH ACTION

The youth of today will be the ones to live through this century's climate change, so what action are they taking to tackle the crisis? They are, inventing, planting, carrotmobbing, recycling and snapping their way into a post-carbon future.

E-WASTE

Fifteen-year-old Alex Lin became interested in electronic waste (e-waste) in 2005 when he learned that more than four million computers, televisions and monitors would be sent to the landfill in his home state of Rhode Island in the USA by 2011. With friends from his home town, he founded an organisation called WIN to try and do something about this madness.

By connecting with local recyclers and installing a permanent collection point at the dump, WIN keeps 2.5 tonnes of e-waste out of the local landfill each month. Instead of recycling the best computers, WIN upgrades them with new hard drives and software, giving them to local students and young people in Sri Lanka, Mexico and Cameroon.

CARROTMOBBING

Carrotmobbing is a new way of getting lots of people (the 'mob') to reward businesses for good environmental behaviour (the 'carrot' as opposed to the 'stick'). The first carrotmob event took place in 2008 in San Francisco, USA, when environmentalist Brent Schulkin arranged for a mob of consumers to visit a grocery shop. The shop had agreed to invest 22 per cent of the day's sales into energy efficiency improvements in the building.

Everybody won. The shop got a massive influx of customers, spending US$10,000 throughout the day, and this resulted in a significant carbon- reducing investment in energy efficiency. Young people across Europe and North America have caught on to the idea, organising their own carrotmob events. Brent hopes to see it go global and help push businesses, big and small, to make cuts in their carbon footprint.

⬇ Awaiting the carrotmob in San Fransisco.

ENVIROCYCLE

The Envirocycle Scrap Wind Turbine, created by UK university student Max Robson (22), is made almost entirely from recycled materials, such as an old bicycle frame and scrap parts from cars. Robson says, 'It's so simple to make, unskilled workers anywhere in the world could easily be taught to build it.' With a maximum output of 11.3 watts, the Envirocycle produces enough electricity to trickle charge a battery that can run lighting or a radio. An idea like this could potentially make access to basic renewable electricity a reality for many people living in developing countries.

PLANT-FOR-THE-PLANET

Inspired by UNEP's Billion Tree Campaign at just nine years old, Felix Finkbeiner co-founded Plant-for-the-Planet in 2007. Based in Germany, his organisation aims to get young people energised about solving the impending climate crisis. Travelling to different parts of Germany every second weekend, organising with schools and youth groups, he hopes to see young Germans plant one million trees by 2010. In 2009, Plant-for-the-Planet had already managed an incredible 300,000 trees throughout the country. Finkbeiner doesn't want to stop there. 'The next goal we have after planting one million trees in Germany,' he says, 'is to plant one million trees in every country in the world.'

YOUTH SNAPS

'I believe that the only way we will solve the climate crisis is through a global grassroots movement and the young global citizens of today are leading the way... Their story has to be told and recorded,' says Dutch/Canadian photographer Robert van Waarden. Since 2007, he has been travelling around the world, camera in hand, documenting what young activists and youth organisations are doing to pressurise our governments into doing whatever it takes to combat climate change. Robert has joined the youth climate movement in Indonesia, the USA, Poland, Canada and Denmark, amongst others. 'Through my images,' he says, 'I hope to connect citizens from different continents and combat any sense of hopelessness by demonstrating the strength of our global movement.'

YOUTH ADVOCACY

Young people are on the front lines in the fight against climate change. They are getting angry, loud and active, raising public awareness and forcing politicians to hear their concerns. And they're doing it in very imaginative ways.

CONFERENCE OF YOUTH

When our world leaders meet at UN climate-change negotiations, young people come from around the world to get involved. At each event, people volunteer to facilitate a Conference of Youth (COY) the weekend before the UN negotiations begin. Here they discuss the issues and strategise for the days ahead. During the negotiations, they track what's going on at the talks, lobby politicians, hold demonstrations and keep up blogs to let their peers know what's going on. These activities have gained the youth movement meetings with governments and COY's have been covered by the media, including the *New York Times* and Reuters.

[To find out more, visit www.ukycc.org]

⬆ Just some of the 500 young people who attended COY in 2008. Photos by Robert van Waarden.

CLIMATE SOLUTIONS ROAD TRIP

With a fleet of alternatively fuelled vehicles, including three electric cars, a biofuel-powered truck and a van running on spent vegetable oil, a team of young Indians launched The Climate Solutions India Road Trip in 2009. Accompanied by the first solar-powered band from the USA, the team drove 3,500 km across India, stopping at cities and villages along the way to raise awareness about climate change and the post-carbon future with concerts and discussion groups.

[Read more about the trip at www.indiaclimatesolutions.com]

⬆ 12,000 young people gather at Capitol Hill in Washington D.C., urging the government to take serious climate action.

POWER SHIFT

Arranged by a coalition of youth-led organisations, Power Shift is one of the biggest annual events for young climate-change activists in the UK, Australia, Canada and the USA. Taking place over several days, Power Shift sees thousands of young people engage in dozens of workshops on climate change, energy, activism and political issues. The highlight of Power Shift is a mass demonstration in front of government buildings, where young people make their demands for a post-carbon future clear. And to celebrate all that hard work, the event closes with a fun concert.

[To find out more, visit www.ukycc.org]

International climate camps

Whether in France, India, Ecuador or the UK, you are bound to find a dedicated group organising 'climate camps' throughout the year. Once a target location is selected, thousands of people set themselves up in tents for up to a week to highlight an issue. In the UK, for instance, climate camps have been held at Heathrow airport to protest against airport expansion.

Other camps have protested coal-fired power plants and urged world leaders to act on climate change at high-profile political events. Climate camps are run as a sustainable community where solar panels provide power, waste is recycled and local, organic food is provided. During the camp, ideas are exchanged, contacts made – and you can even learn how to build a wind turbine.

[Visit www.climatecamp.org.uk]

⬆ Climate camp in London for the 2009 G20 Summit.

Convergence

In 2008, five members of the Australian Youth Climate Coalition travelled 23,500 km from Australia to Poznan, Poland. Instead of a day of air travel, they crossed 11 countries in 40 days by train, bus, taxi and and boat to eventually join 500 other international youth climate activists at the UN climate negotiations in Poznan. The point of the journey was not to reduce emissions (which they did by 40 per cent), but to demonstrate just how time-consuming and expensive it is not to travel by air. Their story emphasises the need to start working hard on our low-carbon transport networks. By 2009, their idea had caught on in an action called Convergence where 5,000 youth and others from around the world travelled overland to the UN climate talks in Copenhagen. [see www.youthclimatecoalition.blogspot.com]

Kids on Strike

Use your talent to raise awareness about climate change and the post-carbon future. Sing it, dance it and act it out with Peace Child's new musical, *Kids On Strike*! Created by young people of the world, it features kids in 2050 remembering how the youth of 2010 were the generation that saved the world from catastrophic climate change. Premiered at the 2008 World Youth Congress in Quebec, Canada, it inspired many participants to translate and perform their own version of the musical.

[The script, songs, scores and backing tracks are all available at: www.peacechild.org.]

Letters from 2050

So we made it! It's 2050 and we're living in the post-carbon future – a world no longer dependent on fossil fuels. It feels great! We led the energy revolution and defeated global warming by voting in courageous leaders, living low-carbon lifestyles and spending our money wisely on carbon-free goods. Looking back from our future in 2050, here's what some of us feel a post-carbon future would feel like...

My birthday, 2050: 66 years old. Looking out of my window here in North Yorkshire, little has changed. I retired to the village where I was born – and found it more welcoming than it was when I was a child. Our electricity comes from a shared micro-generator. We now share everything: lawn-mowers – we have three for the village – cars, tools and workshops. It's a real, sustainable community. I was a teacher – and over a 40-year career, I was thrilled to watch sustainability and global studies taking an increasingly central place in the curriculum – pushed by my students who realised how important it was. When I was young I loved to travel – but I am much happier now, travelling in the carbon-free, subterrene network. It's great! I can get to hug my grandchildren in Australia in three hours!

Tanya Mowbray
UK

5 June 2050. Today, World Environment Day celebrates our conquest of global warming – and nowhere is that victory more visible than here in the village where I was born. We planted 10 million trees, so tall forests now cover what was a drought-scarred landscape when I was a child. Rivers flow, cattle graze, children play – and in the herb gardens, I am growing medicines that heal all common diseases. In my village, everyone is vegetarian, everyone is healthy. There is no drop of plastic – no fossil fuel: everything is solar – the electricity, the stoves, the farm machinery. And everything is shared – the cars, the computers, the school books. And so – today, I celebrate – and yet I shudder when I think back and realise how late we were in getting wise to global warming. Thank you, leaders, for your courage in making the right decisions.

Isaac Musyoka
Kenya

After all the excitement of the New Year with family and friends, I sit back and reflect on those warnings of certain climatic catastrophe we feared 50 years ago. Well? We are still here, standing stronger than ever. We managed to prevent our beautiful island from drowning under rising seas. We moved away from our dependency on our oil and natural-gas industries. As the new Silicon Islands, Trinidad and Tobago supply the world with high-end, Earth-friendly ideas and technologies. In doing so, we have managed to reduce our own carbon emissions and contributed to reducing the world's at the same time. Port-of-Spain remains the hub for economic commerce and is littered with stylish, energy-efficient buildings and transport systems that resemble things I saw in movies as a boy. It's been a lot of hard work but we have managed to adjust our attitudes, changed our world and made it a better place for my grandchildren, and the entire human race.

Richard Lewis

Trinidad

29 March 2050. Yesterday I found the diary I wrote as a girl, 40 years ago. It was funny to read my frustration at how lazy everyone was – not recycling, using the car to run to the store, wasting water, happily accepting polluting factories. What is extraordinary is that most people felt just as angry as me: I just didn't know! Thanks to the initiatives of young people, humanity has changed for good. Factories I remember polluting the environment are now museums, exhibiting things that used to kill the environment – petrol-powered cars, plastic bottles, ridiculous plastic packaging, synthetic clothes. Today everything is clean and electric: public transport runs on solar energy, and most of us cycle, which keeps us healthy.

Andrea Arzaba

Mexico

curriculum links

Since the Rio Earth Summit in 1992, education for sustainable development and climate change has taken on a greater importance. Different countries have adopted different educational programmes to tackle the subjects. Energy Revolution supports many areas of the official English curriculum, especially Science, Geography and Citizenship.

National Framework for Sustainable Schools

Energy Revolution can enhance your work towards fitting into the National Framework for Sustainable Schools. It also offers many opportunities for students to develop their PLTS (personal learning and thinking skills) through a range of activities, games and debates.

The UK government wants all schools to be sustainable by 2020 to prepare young people for a lifetime of sustainable living. The National Framework introduces eight 'doorways' through which schools can explore their sustainability and take practical action to reduce their impact on the world. These doorways are: food and drink; energy and water; travel and traffic; purchasing and waste; buildings and grounds; inclusion and participation; local well-being; global dimension. Energy revolution can support schools' sustainability work, and can help explore all these doorways. For more information, go to the National Framework website:
http: www.teachernet.gov.uk/sustainableschools/framework/

Energy Revolution and Science

The importance of science: *'They learn to question and discuss issues that may affect their lives, the directions of societies and the future of the world.'* The chapters in this book link with several areas in the National Curriculum for Science, including key concepts, range and content, and curriculum opportunities. The table below details the specific areas of the programme of study to which they can be applied.
http://curriculum.qca.org.uk/key-stages-3-and-4/subjects/science/keystage3/index.aspx

Energy Revolution Chapter	Links to Science Key Stage 3
The warming world	1.1, 1.2, 3.4a, 3.4c, 4a, 4d, 4g
Who suffers?	1.2, 3.4c, 4a, 4c, 4d, 4g
Post-carbon power	1.1, 1.2, 3.1, 3.4c, 4a, 4c 4d, 4g, 4i
Transport revolution	1.1, 1.2, 3.1, 3.4c, 4a, 4c, 4d, 4g, 4i
One planet living	1.1, 1.2, 1.3, 3.4c, 4a, 4c, 4d, 4g, 4i
Lawmakers and big business	1.2, 1.3, 4a, 4g, 4i
Acting up	1.2, 1.3, 4c, 4g, 4i

Energy Revolution and Geography

The importance of geography: *'Geography inspires pupils to become global citizens by exploring their own place in the world, their values and their responsibilities to other people, to the environment and to the sustainability of the planet.'* The table below details the areas from the UK Geography programme of study to which this book can be applied.

http://curriculum.qca.org.uk/key-stages-3-and-4/subjects/geography/index.aspx

Energy Revolution Chapter	Links to Geography Key Stage 3
The warming world	1.1, 1.2, 1.3, 1.4, 1.5, 1.6, 1.7, 3a, 3d, 3e, 3f, 3g, 3h
Who suffers?	1.1, 1.2, 1.3, 1.4, 1.5, 1.6, 1.7, 3a, 3d, 3e, 3g, 3h
Post-carbon power	1.2, 1.3, 1.4, 1.5, 1.6, 1.7, 3a, 3d, 3e, 3g, 3h
Transport revolution	1.2, 1.3, 1.4, 1.5, 1.6, 1.7, 3a, 3d, 3e, 3g, 3h
One planet living	1.1, 1.2, 1.3, 1.4, 1.5, 1.6, 1.7, 3a, 3d, 3e, 3g, 3h
Lawmakers and big business	1.2, 1.3, 1.4, 1.5, 1.6, 1.7, 3a, 3d, 3e, 3h
Acting up	1.2, 1.3, 1.4, 1.5, 1.6, 1.7, 3a, 3e, 3g, 3h

Energy Revolution and Citizenship

The importance of citizenship: *'Citizenship encourages pupils to take an interest in topical and controversial issues and to engage in discussion and debate.'* The table below outlines the relevant areas of the Citizenship programme of study in key concepts, key processes, range and content, and curriculum links.

http://curriculum.qca.org.uk/key-stages-3-and-4/subjects/citizenship/keystage3/index.aspx

Energy Revolution Chapter	Links to Citizenship Key Stage 3
The warming world	1.3c, 2.1, 3k, 4a, 4g, 4h
Who suffers?	1.1b, 1.3c, 2.1, 3k, 4a, 4g, 4h
Post-carbon power	1.3c, 2.1, 2.3a, 3e, 3k, 4a, 4g, 4h
Transport revolution	1.3c, 2.1, 2.3a, 3e, 3k, 4a, 4g, 4h
One planet living	1.3c, 2.1, 2.3a, 3e, 3k, 4a, 4h
Lawmakers and big business	1.1d, 1.3c, 2.1, 2.3a, 3a, 3e, 3k, 4a, 4h
Acting up	1.3c, 2.1, 2.3a, 3e, 4a, 4h

Energy Revolution can, of course, be introduced in many other subject areas, most obviously economics, business studies and history.

jargon buster

Adaptation Fund
Established by the Kyoto Protocol to finance adaptation projects such as sea walls, flood defences and more, in developing countries that are particularly vulnerable to the effects of climate change.

biodiversity
The variety of living species in a given ecosystem or on the entire Earth. Often used as a measure of the health of biological systems.

biofuels
Fuel obtained from vegetation: first-generation biofuels are made from sugar, starch, vegetable oil or animal fats; second-generation biofuels come from corn straw, wood and special biomass crops like miscanthus; third-generation biofuel – the most promising – is made from algae.

carbon capture and storage (CCS)
The process of capturing carbon particles emitted by fossil-fuel power plants, liquefying it and storing it underground or under the sea.

carbon footprint
The total greenhouse-gas emissions caused directly and, sometimes, indirectly by individuals, organisations, groups or products.

carbon offsetting
A mechanism of the Kyoto Protocol designed to reduce CO_2 emissions by balancing them by undertaking environmental projects that absorb carbon, such as planting a forest.

Climate Change
Any measurable change in weather patterns over a period of years

climate justice
A process by which those causing climate change are made to pay to help those suffering from it.

concentrating solar power (CSP)
Power stations that work by using mirrors to concentrate sunlight into a single, very hot beam that heats up water to drive turbine generators and make electricity.

development aid
Financial support offered to a country to fund long-term alleviation of poverty.

developing world
Less Economically Developed Countries (LEDCs).

drought
A long period of abnormally low rainfall that adversely affects growing and living conditions for plants and animals.

ecosystem
Nature's way of getting plants, animals, insects and micro-organisms in a defined area working together.

EUMENA
The European Union, the Middle East and North Africa.

European Union (EU)
An economic and political grouping of 27 European countries that believe in democracy and the rule of law, governed by a Commission and an elected European Parliament.

fair trade
A way of trading that ensures disadvantaged farmers and workers in developing countries get a fair and consistent price for their products.

fossil fuel
Nature's one-time gift to mankind – coal, oil and natural gas. Fuels produced by decomposition and compression of vegetation and animals over 200 million years.

geo-engineering
The deliberate manipulation or rebuilding of the Earth's natural infrastructures such as seas, forests, mountains and lakes.

geothermal energy
Energy obtained from heat under the Earth.

global warming
The measurable warming of the surface temperature of the Earth.

greenhouse development rights
The rights accorded to developing nations to advance in a low-carbon way.

greenhouse effect
The process by which the surface temperatures on Earth are raised by a cocktail of greenhouse gases (mainly CO_2) trapping heat from the sun – like a greenhouse.

ground source heat pumps
A device to draw heat from the Earth and compress it, like a refridgerator in reverse, to create heat to warm water for domestic use.

hybrid vehicles
Vehicles such as cars or lorries that use two or more fuel sources to power their engines – like electricity and petrol.

hydroelectricity
Power harnessed from the flow of water.

International Energy Agency (IEA)
Founded during the oil crisis of 1973–74, the IEA is an intergovernmental organisation that provides energy policy advice to its 28 member nations.

mass extinction
A sharp increase in the number of species becoming extinct in a short period of time.

megawatt (MW)
A unit of power equal to one million watts.

nuclear power
Power generated by turbines, driven by water heated by controlled nuclear reactions from splitting atomic particles.

nuclear fusion
A nuclear reaction in which nuclei combine at high temperatures to form bigger nuclei and simultaneously release energy.

ocean acidification
The process by which oceans become more acidic, with decreasing pH levels. Acidification is caused by oceans soaking up carbon dioxide from the atmosphere.

ocean energy
Energy harnessed from waves or tides.

parts per million (of carbon)
A value representing the number of particles of carbon dioxide in the atmosphere.

permafrost
Areas of the Earth that stay below freezing point (0°C or 32°F) for two or more years.

post-carbon future
A time in the future when people have stopped using fossil (carbon-emitting) fuels.

ratify
To give official agreement to a treaty or constitution; usually given by an elected parliament or assembly.

smart grids
Electrical distribution grids that include an Internet data feedback system.

solar photovoltaic cells (PVs)
Panels, usually embedded in glass, that generate electricity when the sun shines on them. Second-generation solar PVs use inks, dyes and thin film.

super-grid
An electrical distribution system that enables large volumes of electricity to be transported across great distances; also called high-voltage DC grids or ultra-high voltage grids.

sustainable
Capable of being continued with minimal long-term effect on the environment.

United Nations (UN)
The international government organisation founded in 1945 to 'save succeeding generations from the scourge of war'. Its 192 member states work together to maintain international peace, promote human rights, sustainable development and a safe, secure world for all.

WWF
World Wide Fund for Nature. One of the world's largest conservation/environmental organisations, founded in 1961.

further information

General

TUNZA Magazine, www.unep.org/Publications/Tunza.asp

  'The Road to Copenhagen,' Vol 7., No. 2

  'Your Planet Needs YOU,' Vol. 7 No. 1

  'CO2 – Kick the Habit,' Vol. 6 No. 1.

www.ourplanet.com

www.treehugger.com

www.bbc.co.uk/bloom/

www.guardian.co.uk/environment

www.postcarbon.org

www.bellona.org

www.wbcsd.org

www.wired.com/science

www.scientificamerican.com

www.newscientist.com

www.worldwildlife.org

www.greenpeace.org

www.worldwatch.org

www.foe.co.uk

www.unfccc.int

www.unep.org/climateneutral

www.panda.org/climate/pocketguide

www.renewableenergyworld.com

www.europeanenergyreview.eu

Section One – Problem: global warming

Mark Lynas, *6 Degrees: Our Future on a Hotter Planet*; www.marklynas.org

www.ipcc.ch

www.co2now.org

www.westcoastclimateequity.org

www.livescience.com/environment

www.newint.org/issues/2009/01/01/

www.christianaid.org.uk

Human Development Report, Climate Change, hdr.undp.org/en/reports/global/hdr2007-2008

Section Two – Solution: a post-carbon future

George Monbiot, *Heat*

www.monbiot.com

www.forumforthefuture.org

home.clara.net/darvill/altenerg/

www.iea.org

www.desertec.org

www.scientificamerican.com/article.cfm?id=asolar-grand-plan

www.betterplace.com

www.whatgreencar.com

www.riversimple.com

www.worldskycat.com

www.bioregional.com

www.energysavingtrust.org.uk

www.masdar.ac.ae

www.iter.org

www.verticalfarm.com

Section 3 – Action: making it happen

www.combatclimatechange.org

www.transitiontowns.org

www.350.org

www.unep.org/billiontreecampaign

www.ukycc.org

www.climatecamp.org.uk

www.youthclimatecoalition.blogspot.com

www.indiaclimatesolutions.com

www.itsgettinghotinhere.org

www.syc-cjs.org/advocacy

www.stopclimatechaos.org

www.climatechangecoalition.org

www.recyclenow.com

www.eco-schools.org.uk

www.growingschools.org.uk

www.postcarbon.org/farm-for-the-future

www.locavores.com

index

Peace Child International

Empowering young people to be the change they want to see in the world

Peace Child is a youth-run British Charity with affiliates in over 120 countries, whose aim is first to INFORM young people about the major challenges they will face in their lifetimes, then train and support them to take ACTION to address those challenges.

Here's a sample of the kind of projects we do:

PUBLICATIONS: Peace Child's global network of young people have written and illustrated, designed and edited over 30 books and lesson plans on complex global issues like sustainable development and human rights. *Energy Revolution* is the third Peace Child book published by Evans Brothers Limited.

DRAMA AND MUSICALS: In the 1980s, PCI promoted its musical, *Peace Child*, to bring together US and Soviet children and pave the way to end the Cold War. In 2009/10, in addition to *Kids on Strike!*, our climate-change musical that accompanies this book, PCI is preparing another new musical to look at multi-faith issues and how religion should unite, rather than divide, people.

EDUCATION PROGRAMMES: PCI runs a schools programme in the UK training young Be the Change! Ambassadors to become effective peer-to-peer educators, delivering workshops, classroom games and Assembly performances on sustainable lifestyles and managing conflict.

WORLD YOUTH CONGRESS: In 1999, PCI launched the World Youth Congress Series to promote a more effective role for young people in development. It brings together young activists working to address the needs of their communities. WYCs are life-transforming events for all who attend them – meeting with other activists from 100+ countries, meeting development professionals, attending skill-sharing workshops and fun cultural programmes. The next is in Istanbul in 2010 and Brazil in 2012. In alternate years, PCI organises the European Youth Congress on issues of interest to young Europeans.

BE THE CHANGE! Promoting Youth-led Sustainable Development: PCI's own YLD programme has supported 300+ YLD projects in 67 countries launching all kinds of initiatives from urban eco-farms in Peru, flood defences in Nigeria, 'Schools for Street Children' in Sierra Leone etc.

Join us!

Volunteer with Peace Child: we have brilliant volunteer opportunities for young people in the UK, in India and elsewhere - in our schools programmes, working on books like this, and our other projects.

Visit: www.peacechild.org - or write: info@peacechild.org - and see how you can get involved in our work

Peace Child International

The White House, BUNTINGFORD, Herts, United Kingdom, SG9 9AH;
e-mail: info@peacechild.org; phone: (+44) 176 327 4459; Fax: (+44) 176 327 4460